私がつなぐ
沖縄のククル心

創価学会沖縄未来部 編

第三文明社

はじめに

　"ありったけの地獄を一つに集めた"と言われるほど、凄惨を極めた沖縄戦。美しい海は軍艦で埋め尽くされ、空襲や艦砲射撃による「鉄の暴風」は、豊かな島の形をも変えました。

　「二度と戦争を起こしてはならない」──この不戦の誓いを胸に、創価学会沖縄青年部は、戦争体験の継承運動を展開してきました。沖縄戦の体験者から聞き取りを行い、一九七四（昭和四十九）年六月、創価学会青年部による戦争体験集の第一号となる『打ち砕かれしうるま島』を発刊。同年二月、沖縄を訪れていた池田大作創価学会会長（当時）は、中学生・高校生の代表と懇談し、次のように語りました。

　「今、戦争の記憶が、社会から忘れ去られようとしている。だからこそ諸君には、二十一世紀のために、お父さん、お母さんたちの戦争の苦しみを、厳然と伝え残すべき使命と責任と義務があります」

1

「戦争も、歳月がたてば真実が忘れられ、歴史のなかに埋もれてしまう。書き残さなければ、真実は伝わらない。だから諸君にも、平和のために、〝沖縄の心〞を伝えるために、戦争体験の証言集を残してほしいというのが、私の願いです」

池田会長の提案を受けた中高生のメンバーは、クラブ活動や勉強の合間を縫い、父母や近隣の人びとに戦争体験を聞いて歩きました。体験者から聞いたあまりにも悲惨な話に、眠れない夜もあったに違いありません。一つの本を作る中で、皆が戦争の醜悪さを胸に刻み、平和建設への誓いを新たにしました。中高生が聞き取りした内容は七六年六月、証言集『血に染まるかりゆしの海』として結実しました。

沖縄戦から七十五年という節目を迎えるにあたり、沖縄未来部は、昨年（二〇一九年）、中高生による戦争体験の聞き取りを実施。十五人の中高生が、八人の戦争体験者から話を聞くことができました。

取材した体験者は、沖縄戦当時、九歳から十九歳の方々です。話を聞いた中高生のメンバーと同年代の時に沖縄戦を体験しています。

「いくさや、ならんどー（戦争はいけない）」。直接聞く体験者の言葉は、私たちの胸に深く迫ってきました。聞き取りを終えたメンバーは皆、「私たちが次代へ平和の思いをつないでいきたい」と決意をしていました。本書では、そうした思いをつづった取材後記も収録しています。また、本書に収められた貴重な証言を世界へ届けようと、全文英訳も付けました。

この証言集が、「二度と戦争を起こしてはならない」との〝沖縄の心〟を後世に伝え、世界平和の連帯を結ぶ一助となれば、これ以上の喜びはありません。

二〇二〇年六月

沖縄未来部長　　　　山口　敬祐
沖縄女子未来部長　　神谷　有希乃

3

沖縄戦略年表

1944年（昭和19年）

3・22	大本営、第32軍（司令官・渡邉正夫中将）を設立
4・15	第32軍、沖縄本島、伊江島、宮古島に航空基地建設を発令
7・7	サイパン陥落
8・10	渡邉司令官に代わって、牛島 満 中将、第32軍司令官に着任
8・22	対馬丸が米潜水艦の攻撃を受け、悪石島付近で轟沈。学童784人を含む1482人（氏名判別者数）が犠牲に
10・10	米軍、南西諸島全域を空襲。那覇市を集中攻撃し、90%が壊滅
12・9	第32軍、首里城地下に司令部壕構築を開始
12・14	第32軍、南西諸島警備要項に基づき沖縄本島中南部在住の老人、女性の北部疎開と戦闘能力のある者の戦闘参加を県に要求

1945年（昭和20年）

2・9	米軍、沖縄侵攻作戦（アイスバーグ作戦）を発令
2・10	島田 叡 知事、中南部住民10万人の北部疎開を指示
3・23	米軍、南西諸島全域を空襲

3・24	米艦隊、沖縄本島砲撃を開始
3・26	米軍、座間味村3島に上陸。慶留間島、座間味島で住民の「強制集団死」発生
3・27	米軍、渡嘉敷島など3島に上陸
3・28	渡嘉敷島で住民の「強制集団死」発生
3月末	沖縄の21の中等学校の生徒が「鉄血勤皇隊」「学徒隊」として戦場に動員
4・1	米軍、沖縄本島西海岸（北谷・読谷村）に上陸
4・3	米軍、沖縄本島を分断。北部方面と南部方面に部隊を展開
4・19	米軍、宜野湾・浦添の防衛戦を突破
5・5	日本軍、総攻撃に失敗。沖縄戦の敗北決定的に
5・22	第32軍司令部、首里城放棄と南部方面への撤退を決定
6・19	第32軍の牛島司令官、「最期まで敢闘し悠久の大義に生くべし」とする最終命令
6・23	牛島司令官が自決
6・25	大本営、沖縄作戦の終了を宣言
8・15	日本が無条件降伏
9・7	南西諸島の日本軍残存部隊と米軍間で降伏調印式

もくじ

本当は記憶から消したい、
十九歳のあの日々を………………

証言者　与那嶺 ツルさん
取材者　與那覇 美月さん

むすびにかえて………………………………

【編集注】

一、証言者の年齢および取材者の学年は、すべて取材時のものです。取材は、
二〇一九年二月から四月にかけて行われました。

一、「集団自決」という言葉について、「自決」には「国に殉ずる崇高な死」
という意味があり、国が起こした戦争のために強制的に死に追いやられ
た一般市民の死にあてはまらないとの観点から、再検討する動きがあり
ます。そこで、本書では特定の地域共同体や家族などが集団で「死を選
択せざるを得なかった」という意味から、「強制集団死」と表現した個
所があります。ただ、証言では、証言者が使用している言葉を尊重し、
そのまま使用しています。

戦争の真実を
伝えるのは難しい
あまりにも残酷すぎるから

▷証言者　糸数 武 さん
いとかず たけし

那覇市在住／86歳

▶取材者　西里 伊吹 さん
にしざと いぶき

高校1年生

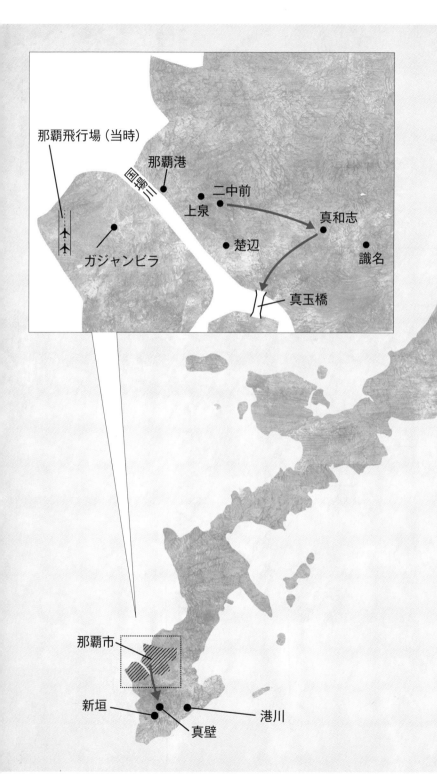

那覇飛行場（当時）

那覇港

国場三

二中前

上泉

真和志

ガジャンビラ

楚辺

識名

真玉橋

那覇市

新垣

真壁

港川

厳しい父と映画好きの母

　私は一九三三（昭和八）年に那覇市の上泉（現在の久茂地）で生まれました。両親が年を取ってから授かった子どもだったので、私の誕生を家族みんなが喜んだそうです。

　両親は盆正月とか、親戚や知人の家に行く時は、必ず私を連れていってくれました。父・昌永は海軍出身の軍人でしたので、厳格で怖い存在。ものすごく厳しく育てられました。喧嘩して泣いて帰ると怒られるので、涙が乾くまで待って家に帰りました。叱られる時は決まって殴られ、当時の軍隊のようでした。ただ、私は文字を書くのが好きで、国語のノートに一生懸命書く練習をすると、今度はすごくほめられました。ほめる時には徹底してほめてくれるのです。

　母・悦子は大の映画好きで、何度か一緒に映画に行きました。その時に人力車に乗るのが私の楽しみでした。そのころの映画館では、軍国主義の時代を反映して、映画の前に軍事ニュースが流れました。日本軍が東南アジアや南方方面で勝利の進軍を続けている様子が紹介されると、観客は大拍手で喜びました。今さらながら思うことは、当時の日本の軍部がいかにわれわれ国民に対し、軍国主義教育を進めていたのかということです。

那覇市の甲辰尋常小学校に入学、その後、四年生の夏に同じ那覇市の楚辺国民学校に転校しました。楚辺のあたりは少し畑も残っていて、学校の敷地内にも大根やにんじん、葉野菜の畑があり、私も水や肥料をやったり、雑草をむしったりといった畑仕事を経験しました。都市部の小学校からの転校でしたが、すぐに友達もできました。

ある時から、輜重兵（軍需品の補給・輸送を担当する兵士）たちが学校にやってきました。彼らは木を切って小屋を作り、馬を養っていました。馬を非常に大事にしていたことが印象に残っています。私たち上級生は、馬小屋の屋根に載せる茅を刈る作業に動員されました。私はそうした作業は未経験でした。もたもたしていると、見かねた農家の同級生たちが私に茅の刈り方を教えてくれました。

学校では、標準語励行のため沖縄の言葉を使うことが禁止されました。うっかり沖縄言葉を使うと、方言札という罰札を首からかけさせられるのです。それはかなりの屈辱感でした。

激しくなる戦況の下で

一九四四（昭和十九）年。私は十一歳、五年生になっていました。二月ごろから、日本

本土への学童疎開が始まりました。疎開は学童と引率の先生たちだけで、親は一緒に行くことができません。親子が離れ離れになるということでした。疎開も終盤になると母子の乗船が許されることになりました。父は、私と母をこの最後のチャンスで鹿児島へ疎開させようとしたのです。母は猛反対しました。たとえどんな危険な目にあっても、家族は一緒にいたほうがいいと言い張り、私たち家族は沖縄残留組になりました。

その年の十月十日。その日はちょうど日曜日で、空は雲一つない青空でした。私は残留組の友達と遊んでいました。十時ごろに飛行機の爆音が聞こえてきました。私たちは近所の子ども二、三人でモクマオウの木によじ登ってその様子を見ていました。友軍による飛行訓練と思っていたのですが、突然、編隊飛行から機銃掃射の白煙が見え、急降下しながら爆撃を始めたのです。

那覇港と那覇飛行場の方向でした。次にガジャンビラ（那覇市金城）の高射砲が一斉に火を噴いたのです。そして、けたたましくサイレンが鳴り響き、

「敵機来襲！　敵機来襲！」と甲高い声が上がりました。私たちは慌てて木から下りて一目散に家に戻りました。

家に着くと、防空頭巾をかぶるのもそこそこに、両親と家の前に掘ってあった防空壕に飛び込みました。日ごろ教わった通りに親指を耳の穴に入れ、残りの指で目を覆いました。

どれくらい時間がたったでしょうか。夕方には空爆がやんだので、恐る恐る壕から這い出て、モグラのように穴から顔を出しました。みんなおっかなびっくりで、一人また一人と壕から出てきました。

私の住んでいた二中前市場の十二軒の家は完全な形で残っていました。それは奇跡でした。那覇の街は燃えていて、まだ危険な状態なので日が暮れてから旧真和志村の識名へ避難のため向かいました。ところが、どこも避難民でごった返して、休めるところなどありません。諦めて家へ戻りました。

住むところを追われ、家族はバラバラに

一九四五（昭和二十）年三月二十三日がやってきました。朝食を食べ終えたころ、はるか遠くでパンパンと太鼓のような音が聞こえました。しばらくすると兵隊が来て、「敵の艦船が、島尻郡の港川方面に艦砲射撃を開始した。多分そこから上陸するのではないか」「ここにいては危険だから、どこか大きな壕へ避難したほうがいい」と言うのです。父も海軍の経験から「ここにいては危ない」と判断し、逃げることになりました。

私は水筒に水を入れ、救急袋を肩に引っかけて出発に備えました。日ごろからそのよう

に教えられていたので、すぐにできました。「逃げなくては」という一心でした。

私たちは家の近くにあった城岳（じょうがく）の壕に入りました。でも一週間くらいして、兵隊から「こっちは軍が作った壕だから出ていってくれ」と言われました。民間人は立ち退（の）かなくてはなりません。そのころから日本兵に意見を言うことは一切できませんでした。地域のまとめ役として区長をやっていた父は、役場にも通じていたので、旧真和志村役場の後ろにある「ニービ壕」に移動することにしました。

そこにはすでに三世帯十二人が避難していました。父と母はその人たちを拝み倒して、やっとの思いでその壕に入れてもらうことができました。その方々はとても親切で、ご飯を分けてくれたり、お茶を入れてくれました。お腹（なか）が空いていた私たちにとって、とてもありがたいことでした。外では戦闘が繰り広げられていましたが、壕の中では心和（なご）む日々を送ることができました。

敵のトンボ（軽飛行機）が日本軍の陣地を見つけると、米軍の軍艦から総攻撃を受けます。艦砲射撃で草木はほとんど吹き飛ばされて、灰色の地肌がむき出しになってしまいました。遠くにあった丘が総攻撃で半分なくなるのを目撃し、私はその様子をじっと見ていました。子どもながらに、これは大変な状況になっていると思いました。周りの大人が話をしてい

るのをじっと聞いていましたが、島中を軍艦が取り囲んでいるとかいう話は、想像をする
ことができませんでした。

艦砲射撃はもちろんのこと、小銃の弾もヒュウヒュウと飛んでくるようになりました。
海軍の経験を持つ父はその音を敏感に察知して、「米軍がすぐ近くまで迫っている」と皆
に伝えました。米軍の捕虜になるよりも、島尻方面へ逃げたほうがいいという結論が出て、
全員で逃げることになりました。

ところが、出発間際になって、父のお腹の具合が悪くなり、母と私に「皆さんと先に行
きなさい、後で追っていくから」と言うのです。母と私は父の具合が良くなるまで待つと
言ったのですが、皆さんの迷惑になるからと聞きません。押し問答の末、「それでは先に
行くから、早く来てよ」と母は壕の仲間の後を追いました。その言葉が母との別れとなり
ました。私はどちらと一緒に行くか迷いましたが、具合の悪い父を一人にできずに残りま
した。三十分ほどして、父と二人で後を追って歩き出しました。ところが、すぐに追いつ
けると思っていたのに、なかなか追いつくことができません。

那覇と南部をつなぐ真玉橋は、たくさんの避難民が集まっていました。ここで国場川を
渡らないと南部へ逃げることができないのです。橋は日本軍の手によって二カ所が壊され

ていました。父が私の手を握って、破壊された橋を上ったり下りたりしながら対岸へと渡りました。母とはこのへんで会えるだろうと思っていました。

周りでは、離れ離れになった家族を探して、たくさんの人が大声で名前を呼んでいました。私はたまらなくなり、「お母さん、お母さん」と叫びました。「糸数悦子」と母の名前を大きな声で叫びました。ところが「そんな大声で呼ぶな、急いで逃げろ」と兵隊に怒鳴られます。「まごまごせずに行きなさい」と日本軍に追い払われ、諦めるしかありませんでした。真和志村の壕を出て母はどこへ行ったのか……。母とはそれっきり会うことができませんでした。

あまりに残酷な、戦争の真実

逃げるといっても、はっきりした目的地があるわけではありません。とにかく南部へ、みんなが逃げるところについていくんです。一人二人ではなく、グループになって逃げていきます。食料がないので、芋を手で掘って食べたり、葉っぱも我慢して食べました。夜に水を汲みに行って飲んでいましたが、明るくなってみると、そこにはたくさんの人が死んでいたということもありました。

道端で亡くなっている人たちもたくさん見ました。人間が死んでガスが発生すると、体が子牛くらい大きくなります。想像できますか？　間違ってそこを踏んでしまうと、体の皮がぺろっとむけて、死んだ人の臭いが体について落ちないんです。爆風で吹き飛ばされて、体の半分だけが木に引っかかり、手がぶらりとしている、そんな光景も見ました。それを見ても、「自分たちもこんなふうになるのかな」としか思わなかったです。そういう体験をしたからでしょうか。今でも人が亡くなっても、怖く感じないのです。

ある時、私たちの近くに爆弾が落ちました。一緒に逃げていた二十代の女の人が、背中にいっぱい破片が当たって、ずっと唸っていました。朝まで唸って、とうとう亡くなってしまいました。心ある人たちが、爆弾で地面に開いた穴にその人の亡骸を置いて、土をかぶせていました。命がけで逃げている途中に、すごい人たちがいるなと感動をしました。

私は、とにかく、生きながらえるにはどうするかということしか頭にありませんでした。それしか考えることができなかったのです。私も至近弾をくらいました。自分にも何か当たったような気がしました。しばらくしてから、痛みが来ました。弾はお尻から入って、その時は痛みを感じませんでした。腿の内側を抜けていました。父はすぐに私が大事に持ってきた救急袋から、ヨードチンキを出して塗り、応急処置をしてくれました。

戦場で、生きている人間にうじがわいているのを初めて見ました。信じられないことに、その人は自分の腕のうじを竹の枝をお箸にして取っていました。私は薬のおかげで傷口が化膿せず、うじはわきませんでした。足が痛いので普通に歩けない感じでしたが、後遺症もなく歩けました。

逃げ込んだ壕で、「五分以内に立ち退かないと殺す」と言って銃口を向ける日本兵がいました。子ども心に、兵隊なのになぜ誰も守らないんだと憤りました。

戦闘の真っただ中にいて、砲弾にやられるか、友軍にやられるか……。私は生きるという希望を失っていました。戦争はこんなものなのかと冷静に見ていました。

父との別れ

六月中旬ごろには真壁、新垣あたりまで来ていました。一段と激しい艦砲射撃がこの一帯を襲っていました。壕の中にいても、耳をつんざくような爆音が響いていました。

岩を掘った頑丈な壕を見つけて、父子二人だからと頼み込んで隠れていました。壕に入れない人たちは民家や屋敷の石垣に板などをかぶせて、しのいでいる状態でした。近くに、民家の石垣にトタンをかけて、土をかぶせて隠れているおばあさんたちがいました。艦砲

の攻撃がゆるくなった時に、「腕を怪我した人がいるので、手当てをしてくる」と、父は私の救急袋を持って飛び出していきました。十分後に再び激しい艦砲射撃がありました。同じ穴に隠れていた人たちが、艦砲射撃がやんでも、父は帰ってくる気配がありません。

様子を見に出ていき、戻ってくると、「お父さんはあっちにいるけど返事をしなかったよ」

「見に行ってきたら」と言うのです。その瞬間、ひょっとしたら父に何か起こっているのではという予感がありました。その場所に行くと、石垣にもたれかかった父がいました。

「お父さん、お父さん」と呼びかけても返事はありません。揺すっても返事がないのです。

その時、ハッとしました。父の体は冷たくなっていました。私はそれで、父が亡くなったんだとわかりました。

みんなのところに戻って、壕の中で大きな声で泣きました。周りの人は父の死を知っていたのでしょう。「もしあんたが死んでいたら、お父さんは生きても仕方なかったはずだよ。あんたが生きていれば、お父さんの弔いができるじゃないか」と話をしてくれました。

私は悲しさと不安で胸がいっぱいになり、涙が止まりません。母とは別れたきりです。一人ぼっちになった私を、壕の中の人たちが精いっぱい励ましてくれました。

父にしがみついて、戦場をここまで生きてきたのです。

不思議と父の亡くなった次の日から砲撃はピタリとやみ、艦砲が飛んでくることはありませんでした。その日は朝から晴天で、太陽がとても眩しく感じられました。

父が死ぬ前の日の夜のことを、今でも思い出します。艦砲射撃がやみ、米軍が小休止の時間になったのを見計らって、父は私を連れて外に出ました。壕の裏側の小高い土手に腰を下ろして二人で天を見上げました。それは久しぶりに見る星空でした。

父はゆっくりと話しました。「武、今からお父さんが言うことをしっかり聞いておきなさい。もし、戦争に負けて米軍の捕虜になった場合、大人は殺すかもしれないけど、子どもは殺さないと思う。それでも苦しい責めにあったら、一番簡単で苦しまずに死ぬ方法を教えておく。眠れるように死ねるから」と。私はうなずきました。そして、父は私を抱きしめてくれたのです。避難が始まってから、それまでにないことでした。父はなぜ死ぬことを自分に話したのだろうと、不思議でなりませんでした。

捕虜となってからの日々

その後、浜松出身のお医者さんと一緒にいました。距離にして百メートルほど先を、戦車が通りました。戦車の後ろにいたアメリカ兵が私たちを見つけて飛んできました。私は

立ち上がり逃げようとしましたが、お医者さんがズボンをつかんで引き倒ししました。「動いてはいけない。じっとしていなさい」と。

アメリカ兵は携帯食料（レーション）をくれました。私が、中にあるビスケットを食べようとしたら、お医者さんは「ちょっと待って」と警戒しました。毒味をするかのようにそれを食べて見せました。それを見て私たちも安心し、ビスケットを食べました。その時は、こんなにおいしいお菓子があるのかという気持ちでした。その日、私は捕虜になりました。捕虜になって車に乗せられるその時に、「自分は生き延びたのだ」と実感しました。

捕虜になった後、何カ所かトラックで移動させられました。収容所で隊列に並ばされる時も、一人で並んでいました。父の友人の石橋（いしばし）さんでした。「君一人か？ お父さんは？」と聞かれ、「父は死にました」「母ははぐれてわかりません」と答えました。石橋さんは「そうか、それじゃあ私たちと一緒に行こうよ」と言ってくれました。

石橋さんは父が区長をしていた時の知人で、一緒に家を訪ねたことがありました。戦争の前、石橋さんの家で私が踊りを披露（ひろう）したことを覚えていてくれていました。

それからは石橋さんと一緒に過ごすようになりましたが、最初はうれしいとか悲しいとかそういう気持ちもなく、ただ「知らない人ではないから」というだけでした。

収容所を出て那覇に戻ってからも、石橋さんは私をそばに置いてくれました。小学校五年から高校まで教育を受けさせてくれた育ての親です。

石橋さんは私が肩身の狭い思いをしないようにと、いろいろ教えてくれました。芋の取り方、カズラの切り方。石橋家は那覇に田畑もあり、ヤギも飼っていたので、草刈りしたり、薪割りや家畜の世話をしたり、毎日使う水をドラム缶に溜めたりと、忙しく働きました。楚辺での小学校時代に教えてもらった草刈りが、ここで活かされることとなったのです。

おかげで、私は戦争孤児である引け目など全く感じることなく、父と縁ある方の家で育てられました。私は恵まれているとさえ思っていました。戦後お世話になった石橋さんへは感謝しかありません。そして、今の私が存在しているのは、父母がいるからです。今でも両親に感謝の日々を送っています。

西里 伊吹 さん

私は、糸数さんから戦争体験の話を聞いて、今、自分が置かれている状況と、戦争から逃げ、心が休まることがなかった糸数さんの状況の違いに驚きました。それは私の日常——朝、昼、晩、毎日おいしい食事ができて、学校で学べて、好きなスマホを見て楽しんで、という日々とは、あまりにかけ離れていると感じて衝撃を受けました。

話を聞いていく中で、私も知っている地名、二中前や真和志などが多く出てきたので、「あそこで恐ろしい戦争があったんだな」と想像することができました。

夜、軍が休憩していて安全な時に水飲み場に行くと暗くて何も見えなかったけど、明るくなってからそこの前を通ると死体が多くあり、朝と夜では目にうつる景色が違ったという話は、想像するだけで恐ろしい情景です。また、糸数さん自身が銃で撃たれたことに後で気づいた話や、道端でガラスの破片が背中にささって「助けて」と叫んでいる人が次の日には死んでいたことなど、悲惨な体験を聞いて、とてもかわいそうで、どうしようもない気持ちになりました。

「お父さんとお母さんを大切に」「世界のいろんなところで戦争が起こっているけど、戦争では失うものしかないから、平和な世の中にしないといけない」という糸数さんの話が心に残っています。今日、糸数さんから聞いた話を忘れることなく、しっかりと心に刻んで生きていこうと思いました。

今日まで
生きてこられた
奇跡に感謝

▷証言者　**高安 ハツ子** さん
沖縄市在住／89歳

▶取材者　**金城 翔** さん
高校1年生

廣瀬 心優 さん
中学1年生

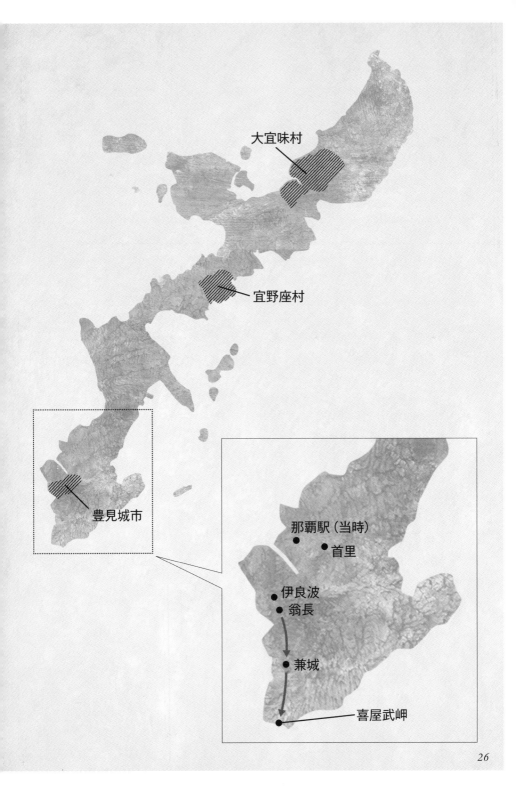

大宜味村

宜野座村

豊見城市

那覇駅（当時）
首里

伊良波
翁長

兼城

喜屋武岬

楽しみだった手伝い仕事

私が第二豊見城尋常小学校の五、六年生のころから、戦争が始まろうとしていました。

沖縄を守るために、日本の兵隊がたくさん入ってきました。大きな家や学校には兵隊が入り、沖縄の山のあちこちを掘って防空壕を造っていました。防空壕造りは、松の木で枠を作って、土が落ちてこないようにします。私たち上級生は、松の皮をはいだり、兵隊が掘った穴の土を外に運んだりして手伝いました。

学校では勉強できませんでした。私は今でも自分の名前しか書くことができません。そういう時代だったのです。

本島南部の豊見城村翁長の農家に生まれました。かやぶき屋根の家に暮らしていました。家族は父と母と兄と妹、弟が三人。おじいさん、おばあさんもいました。

昔は、子どもでもたくさんの手伝い仕事がありました。イー（イグサ）という材料を細く切って干し、ムシロを作りました。それは女性の仕事でした。夜には、ムシロを作るために必要な紐を作りました。

手伝いは大変で嫌になることもありましたが、楽しみでもあったんです。私は洗濯が好

きで、よく川に洗濯をしに行きました。戦前の楽しみは、そういう家の手伝いなどでした。

戦争に備えて、家の西側に防空壕を掘り、食料もちゃんと保管していました。おばあさんがお芋を炊いて、防空壕で食べた思い出もあります。

戦争が来る前にこんなことがありました。天の星に異変が出たんです。星に長い尻尾がついている「いりがんぶし（ほうき星）」のようなものが見えました。白髪のおばあさんが「いりがんぶしがいじとーさー。いくさがちゅーさー。でーじなとーさー（ほうき星が出ているね。戦争がやってくる。大変だ）」と言いました。ほうき星が出る時は、何かよくないことが起きる前触れだと言って、おばあさんが子や孫のことを心配していたことを覚えています。

バラバラになっていく家族

一九四五（昭和二十）年の三月ごろと思います。母が乳飲み子の弟と妹を連れて、本島北部の大宜味村へ疎開することになりました。朝四時に起きて、馬車いっぱいに食べ物などの荷物を積んで、那覇の駅まで見送りに行きました。母との別れはさびしかったけれど、仕方のないことです。

十五歳の私と十三歳と五歳の弟は疎開せずに、豊見城の家に残りました。十七歳の兄は防衛隊に召集されていました。

おばあさんは兄のことを一番気にかけていました。そんな兄が、部隊から逃げて帰ってきたのです。「戦争は負けている。もうどうしようもない。逃げたほうがいいと思って、僕は逃げてきたよ」と。部隊では今日は誰が死んだという話ばかりで、首里方面へ行って、生きて帰ってくるものは誰もいないということでした。兄が逃げて帰ってきたことをおばあさんは大変に喜んで、「家族全員で逃げられる」「もう思い残すことはない」と言って泣いていました。

しばらくは防空壕にいましたが、首里が全滅になるとの話があり、家族で逃げることになりました。今思えば、あの時、防空壕から出なければ良かったと思います。どこへ行っても、島中が戦場でした。でもその時は、どこかに逃げなければ助からないと思っていたのです。

父は五歳の弟をおぶって、私と弟の手を引いてくれました。兄が荷物を担ぎ、私たち家族は南へと逃げました。

最初に親戚のおばさんがいる糸満の兼城に行きました。そこには頑丈に造られた壕があ

りました。しかし、家族全員が壕に入ることができるほど広くはありません。雨あられのように砲弾が落ちてくる中を、年寄りを歩かせるのはかわいそうだからと、おじいさんとおばあさんだけは、そこに置いてもらうことにしました。そのことを、二人にはだまっていました。そして、歩けるもので南の喜屋武へ向かいました。

後で聞かされたのですが、私たちが出た後、「孫たちはどこへ行った」と祖父母は追いかけたそうです。しかし、どうすることもできません。こうして、少しずつ家族がバラバラになっていきました。

逃げ惑う日々

本島最南端の喜屋武には、壕など隠れるところはほとんどありませんでした。兵隊や民間人と多くの避難民で溢れ、お祭りのような人の群れでした。そこをめがけて、爆撃、迫撃砲、艦砲射撃が容赦なく降り注ぎます。逃げ惑う人の波に押されながら、私たち家族も必死になって逃げました。

夜は木の根っこに身を寄せて寝ました。次の日は豚小屋に身を寄せました。父と兄がどこからか戸板を外して持ってきて、小屋の上にかぶせ、その上に木をかぶせて偽装しま

た。

そこに何日いたか、覚えていません。一週間ほどでしょうか。とにかく、海からは艦砲射撃、空からは弾が落ちてきて、生きた心地がしませんでした。どこへ行ったら助かるだろうかと、あっちに逃げたり、こっちに逃げたり。豚小屋の中に隠れている時に、私にも弾の破片が当たりました。太腿に何か熱いものが当たった感覚があり、叩いてはらおうとしたら、弾の破片でした。周りの人は頭や肩に当たっていましたが、不思議と家族は全員無事でした。

いとこ家族には女の子がいたのですが、怖いのですぐに泣き出してしまいます。泣き声が外に漏れると見つかってしまうので、いつも口にボロ布を押し込まれていました。食料もありませんでした。畑からさとうきびを取ってかじりました。豆に砂糖をまぶしたお菓子のようなものも食べました。父のいとこが死ぬ直前に、砂糖湯という芋くずを水で溶いて砂糖を溶かしたものを飲ませてあげました。せめてものという気持ちからです。井戸の水汲みは兄さんがやってくれました。井戸の周囲には、膨れ上がった真っ黒の死体がごろごろしていました。当時は、うず高く積まれた死体を見ても恐ろしいとは感じませんでした。ただ、恐ろしいのは自分が死ぬことでした。どこにいても生きた心地はしま

せんでしたが、不思議と、人が寄り集まっていれば少し安心できました。

父は腎臓の持病があり、ぜーぜーと荒い息をしてつらそうな中、「心配しないでいいよ、

大丈夫だよ」と子どもたちを励ましてくれました。

生まれて初めて見たアメリカ兵

追われて、逃げて、家族は断崖絶壁の喜屋武岬にたどり着いていました。もう目の前には海しかありません。逃げるところがないんです。落ちて死ぬしかないのか……。死ぬのは怖いので、私は岸壁のアダンの木の茂みに隠れました。アダンの葉っぱのトゲにさされても痛いとは感じませんでした。絡みあって生い茂る木の幹の間に、私たち家族はそれぞれ縮こまって入っていました。

雨が夜通し降り注ぎ、機銃掃射の弾がバンバン飛んできます。私の数センチ横を弾がかすめ、爆風で飛んだ土が私にかかりました。それでも私はじっと耐えました。耳と目を押さえて、じっと閉じこもっていました。

どのくらいたったでしょうか。あたりが静かになりました。みんなは生きているだろうかと、あたりをキョロキョロ見回しました。家族みんなが茂みから顔を出しました。あり

がたいことに、全員無事でした。

アダンの茂みに鉄兜をかぶった兵隊が入ってきました。「日本の兵隊が助けに来たんだ！」と喜んで見ると、鼻は高いし、目は青い。生まれて初めて見るアメリカ兵でした。

「出てこい、出てこい」と声をかけています。父が「出よう」と言って、全員茂みから出ていきました。

外に出ると兄は兵隊ではないかと疑われ、念入りに体を調べられていました。私たち家族はそこで捕虜になりました。その日はずっと雨が降っていました。

その時、米兵は生まれたばかりの赤ちゃんを抱っこしていました。この子を連れていきなさいと私たち家族に赤ちゃんを託したのです。自分たちがどうなるかもわからない状況で、赤ちゃんを育てることはできません。米兵の目を隠れて、そっと道のそばに置いてきました。今思えば残酷なことですが、そうするしかなかったのです。親を亡くした子どもたちが、見知らぬ大人の後を追いかけて、泣いている姿もありました。

私の家族は本当にまれな例だった

喜屋武の製糖工場の広場には、捕虜になった人が集められていました。頭から血を流し

ている人、腕がもげている人、体に穴が開いている人と、多くの負傷した人がいました。そんな凄惨な場面を見ても、なんとも思いませんでした。

私たち家族は米軍の大きなトラックに乗せられて、豊見城の伊良波の畑の真ん中に置かれました。男と女、子どもに分けられ、父と兄はどこかへ連れていかれました。とうとう家族が引き離されてしまい、私は金網のそばで「おとうーよー、おとうーよー」と呼びましたが、返事はありません。これから親と一生涯別れて暮らすのかと、夜通し泣きました。

兄は捕虜になるとすぐにハワイに連れていかれたそうです。父は本島北部の宜野座に連れていかれていました。私と弟も、南部の島尻から北部の宜野座の収容所に移送されました。そこで無事に父と再会できました。

母たちも同じ収容所に来ているようだと知り合いから聞かされて、父が探しに行き、やっと家族が一緒に暮らすことができました。母は随分と痩せていました。川に水浴びに行った時、母の肋骨の骨は数えられるほど浮き出ていて、骨と皮だけでした。母は疎開した本島北部の山中で、大変に苦労したことがにじみ出ていました。

それからしばらくして、南部の地元に帰ることになりました。地元の豊見城では共同で畑を耕し、芋などを作りました。軍からも缶詰などの配給がありましたが、それだけでは

足りませんでした。

島尻は激戦地でしたので、家族全員が亡くなり、家の屋号だけしか残っていないところがいっぱいありました。私の家族は、祖父夫婦、父母、父の兄夫婦と弟夫婦、全部で四所帯。全員無事でした。終戦直後、「こんなのはまれだ、珍しい」と言われていました。

戦後、捕虜になった場所に息子たちと一緒に行きました。あの鉄の暴風の中、吹き飛ばされることもなく、怪我(けが)することもなく、生きていたことが珍しいことだと思います。こうして九十歳近くまで生きてきたことを実感し、感謝しました。戦争は二度とあってはならないことなのです。

● 取材を終えて

金城 翔 さん

㊙ はこれまで、小学校、中学校で、平和についての講演会を聞いたり、平和祈念資料館に行ったりして、何度も戦争につい

て学んできました。自分の祖母から体験を聞こうとも思いましたが、祖母が戦争を体験したのは、祖母がまだ三、四歳のころで、そこまではっきりとしたことは覚えていないようでした。そのため、当時を鮮明に覚え

ている戦争体験者の方から直接お話を聞けることは、私にとって大変貴重なものになりました。

高安ハツ子さんが戦争を体験したのは、今の私より若い年齢の時でした。今日も明日も、いつ死ぬかわからない不安な環境の中、それでも生き延びようとしてきた「あの日」とは違い、自分たちのように裕福で安心して過ごすことができる今の日々が、いかに幸せなことであるかを思い知りました。

戦争体験を話している時の高安さんの表情は、とてもつらそうに見えました。七十年以上たった今でも、あのころのことをはっきりと覚えていて、忘れられないのだと気づき、いかに戦争が恐ろしく残酷なものであるかを、あらためて思い知りました。でも、

高安さんが今、幸せそうに暮らしていて、一番つらい経験をした人が一番幸せになっている姿を見て、良かったとも思いました。

今、私たち若い世代に託されていることは、これからも、この戦争について真剣に学び、考え、未来へ伝えていくことだと思っています。貴重な体験をさせていただき、ありがとうございました。

廣瀬 心優 さん

㊙

　は、今まで戦争について本を読んだり、学校の平和学習などで沖縄戦を学んだことがありますが、今回、実際に戦争を体験した方から近い距離で話を聞くということで、とても緊張していました。

高安さんに会った時、「たいした話じゃないんだけど、聞きに来てくれてありがとうね」と私の頬に触れて、優しく話しかけてくれました。私も緊張がとけ、まるで私の本当のおばあさんに話を聞くような気持ちになりました。

高安さんは、沖縄戦があった時のことを今でもはっきりと覚えているようで、詳しく話してくれました。その内容は、優しい声からは想像ができないようなとても怖い体験でした。

敵から身を隠すためにアダンの木の下に隠れたり、足元に転がる銃弾から熱さを感じたり、周りにはたくさんの死体が転がっていたり、生きていたとしても体に大きな怪我（けが）を負った人がたくさんいたそうです。

ほかにも夜中に畑の真ん中に米兵に連れていかれ、置いてけぼりにされたり、親と離れ離れにされたりなど、「今の私と同じ年ごろにこんなことがあるなんて」と、自分に置き換えて考えると、本当にすごく怖くなりました。

高安さんの話を聞いていると、生きていることがすごい」と強く感じました。

普段は、「命」とか「生きる」とか「戦争」について深く考えることがなかったけれど、高安さんの話を聞くことで、私のひいおじいちゃんや、ひいおばあちゃんが守った命があったから今の私があることを感じました。高安さんの家族も三月に十三人目のひ孫が生まれるとうれしそうに話している姿

を見て、私もすごくうれしくなりました。
今回、このような話を聞くことができて、
とても勉強になりました。私たちは実際に
戦争を体験していないけれど、教えても

・・・・・・・・・・・・・・・・・・

らったことを、私のずっと先の家族に伝え
ていけるように、まずは日々の勉強など、一
つ一つ頑張っていきたいと思います。

どんなことがあっても、
戦争だけは
やってはいけない

▷証言者　**屋比久 次郎** さん
（やびく　じろう）
那覇市在住／89歳

▶取材者　**仲里 昌晴** さん
（なかざと　まさはる）
高校2年生

　　　　　与座 万里花 さん
（よざ　まりか）
中学2年生

那覇市街図

明治橋
垣花
識名園
二中前
上間
ガジャンビラ

那覇市
南城市

上間
船越
富里
国吉
富盛
安里・玻名城
慶座絶壁
新垣
摩文仁

学校に行っても、作業しかしなかった

　私のふるさとは真和志村上間（現在の那覇市）です。上間は小高い丘陵地帯で、のどかな農村でした。真和志村字上間の屋比久小というところで誕生し、家族はおじいさん、おばあさん、両親、おじいさんの妹の大おばあさん、お姉さんが一人、兄は三人、一番下は妹でしたが、小さいころに亡くなりました。

　真和志国民学校初等科（現在の小学校）を卒業するまで、暮らしは安定していました。教室も兵隊が使い、初等科六年の夏休みに、学校は兵隊でいっぱいになっていました。初等科の卒業式もガジュマルの木の下で授業を行いました。生徒は、学校の大きなガジュマルの木の下でした。

　高等科（現在の中学校）に入ってからは、学校へ行っても朝から夜までずっと作業で、本なんか一度も読んだことはなかったです。

　ある日、先生に「明日は弁当と、げんのう（金槌）を持ってきなさい」と言われたので、持っていきました。すると、今日からは作業に行くと言うのです。「勝って来るぞと勇ましく」と軍歌を歌いながら、二中前を通り、明治橋を渡って、小禄のガジャンビラ、

垣花（かきのはな）というところまで行きました。一時間以上は歩いたと思います。そこでは兵隊が大きい袋を持ってきて、「五人一組でこの袋に石を集めなさい」と言いました。セメントと石と混ぜて機関砲の陣地を造るのです。集めて置いておくと、別の兵隊が持っていくという作業でした。三十〜四十人の男ばかりで、毎日この陣地構築の仕事をしました。

一九四四（昭和十九）年十月十日。「十・十空襲」が起こりました。この空襲で那覇の港や空港がやられました。午後になって、那覇が全部燃えているのが、上間の高台からも見えました。

そのころは、お墓を開けて防空壕（ごう）にしていました。上間は日本軍の陣地で、今の識名園（しきなえん）のところに野戦病院の大きい壕がありました。高射陣地の部隊に、私のおじさんが家を貸していました。空襲の後は小禄の陣地構築に行くことはなくなり、自分たちの地域で兵隊たちが壕を掘るのを加勢しました。

私が高等科一年の時には海軍の志願兵募集があり、同級生が三人志願していきました。上間にミニ戦車が来た時に、十七、八歳で軍服を着たかっこいい兵隊を見て憧れ、親に内緒で勝手に願書を出しましたが、召集されることはありませんでした。あのころは、戦争で死んだら名誉

学校では、藁人形（わら）を立てて、竹やりで突いて練習しているのを見ました。

空襲から逃げ惑う日々

沖縄の空襲が始まったのは三月二十三日のことです。私の卒業式の朝でした。それから

は毎日空襲です。卒業式は開かれることはなく、卒業証書はもらえていないままです。

その日から夜も戸を閉めて、灯りが外に漏れないように生活していました。上間は高台

で海が見えます。光が漏れたらすぐに艦砲射撃の標的にされるのです。

壕に入っていたら石部隊（陸軍第六十二師団の通称）の兵隊が来て、「明日から石部隊が入

るから、あなたたちは出なさい」「残る者はスパイと見なす」と言ったのです。スパイと

見なされた人は、みんな殺されていました。私たちは仕方なく、安全な壕を出ることにし

ました。壕を追い出された時は、つらかったです。

空襲がやんだ夕暮れにおばあさんたちを連れて、四十〜五十人くらいで一緒に逃げまし

た。壕から出る時は、荷物や食べ物をバーキ（かご）に入れて持って出ました。夜通し歩

と言われていて、死ぬのは怖くないと思っていたのです。ところが、一緒に志願した人の

話を聞くと、「爆弾を持って飛び出して、戦車に体当たりして死んでいる」と言うんですよ。

戦争というのは、人間と人間の殺し合いです。今考えたら、本当にばからしい考えでした。

いて玉城村（現在の南城市）の船越というところに着いたのは、朝五時ごろです。岩陰などにそれぞれに隠れようとしたのですが、雨が降っていたので、老人たちにはきついだろうと、富里まで行き、そこの空き家で休むことにしました。避難して誰もいない家で休みました。

空き家で休んでいる時、艦砲射撃の爆風で、おばあさん、姉の長男、叔母とその子ども三人、いとこ親子の九人、村の人も合わせて多数の人が殺されました。生き残った者は、さらに南へ向かいました。

富里から二日くらい歩いて、島尻の新垣に着きました。壕などはなかったので、人の屋敷にある木の下枝を刈って、その下に隠れました。一週間くらい隠れていました。それから、国吉という集落まで行こうとした時、ワーワーと泣きながら、女性たちが走って逃げてきました。

子どもたちの手を引いて女性がどんどん歩いてくるんです。みんなワーワー泣いていました。米軍のバクナー中将が戦死した報復で、男だけを並べて全員殺したという話を後で聞きました。父が「りっかりっか（さあ、行こう）」とみんなを促して、さらに逃げました。

あたりに赤ちゃんの泣き声が響いていました。心配して見に行くと爆風に吹き飛ばされ

て、誰もいません。赤ちゃんだけそのまま放置されていました。かわいそうですが、戦場では考える暇がないのです。自分もいつ死ぬかわからない状態ですから。

生きるという希望はなかった

新垣では一緒に逃げていた人が十三人も亡くなりました。上からトンボグワー（小型偵察機）が来て合図をすると、すぐに艦砲が飛んでくるんです。丸くなって座っていたその真ん中に爆弾が落ちました。目を開けると、目の前にいた家族が爆風で吹き飛ばされていないんです。母は頭を負傷して、亡くなりました。涙も出ないです。埋葬のための穴を掘るのも大変なので、父が土を少しかぶせました。それが母との別れでした。

そこから摩文仁のほうへ移動しました。そのころになると、米軍の飛行機から投降勧告のビラが落ちてくるようになりました。「男は殺される」と聞いていたので、姉さんと一緒に捕虜になる場所に行きました。ところが、アメリカ兵が立っているのを見た時、「どうせ死ぬんだったら、お父さんのところに行って一緒に死のう」という気持ちが湧き上がりました。姉は「こっちへおいで」と呼びとめましたが、私は必死で父のところへ戻りました。

男ばかり八人が残りました。慶座絶壁（ギーザバンタ）の険しい崖を、帯や着物を結んで下りて行きました。崖の下は、たくさんの死体の山でした。転んだら、死んだ人の上にのしかかる状態です。上を見ると、崖から飛び降り、木に引っかかったまま死んだ遺体がたくさんありました。

悪臭を放つ状況だったはずですが、臭いの感覚がなく、五感は麻痺していました。いとこは新垣で負傷して歩けない状態でした。父がおぶって浜まで下りたのですが、力尽きたのか「もう置いていってくれ」と言い出しました。私たちは鰹節を割って持たせ、岩のそばで別れました。そのまま亡くなったと思います。

サンゴ礁の岩はゴツゴツと尖っていて、裸足だと痛くて歩けません。着ていた着物をさいて足に巻いて歩きました。米軍が船からもマイクで「出てきなさい」と言っていましたが、殺されると思っていたので逃げ続けました。そのころは生きるという希望はなかったのです。いつ死ぬのかということが問題でした。

安里（あさと）・玻名城（はなしろ）のあたりまで来ました。昼はさとうきび畑の中に隠れて、まるでネズミがかじるみたいに、さとうきびをかじっていました。夜になるたび、自分たちの村に帰ろうと歩きました。二、三日歩いて富盛（ともり）まで来た時で

す。日本兵が畑から出てきて「ここは危ないから注意が必要だ」と一列になって歩くことにしました。照明弾がポンポンと上がり、前から機関銃でバラバラと撃たれて四人亡くなりました。私の目の前にいたおじさんも、後ろにいた人も撃たれて亡くなりました。生き残った私たちは、さとうきび畑に入って夜を待とうと休んでいる時に、米兵に見つかりました。私たちは手を上げて畑から出ました。その時は、疲れ果てて、もう弾に撃たれてもいいという気持ちでした。

米兵がケースグワァ（ケースに入った携帯食料）をくれました。開けるとお菓子が入っています。一週間くらいは何も食べていなかったので、それを全部食べました。あの時は本当になんとも言えないくらい、おいしかったことを覚えています。

今でも夜中に目がさめる

自分たちの村は全てが焼けて、家は一軒も残っていませんでした。わが家は、父、兄、私の男三人が生き残りました。そこに復員したおじさんたち三人が加わった男所帯です。家を作って生活を始め、畑をすぐに耕しました。

私は炊事担当になりました。近所に住むお姉さんに習って、米の中に芋を切って入れて

炊くとみんな喜んで食べてくれました。そのころは「戦果」と言って、米軍倉庫から毛布やタオルを盗んでは、芋や米と交換して生活の足しにしていました。

父たちは遺骨を拾いに南部に行く日が多く、二、三日は帰らないこともありました。父は母の遺骨を探し当て、母を供養することができました。

私は今でも、戦争のことを思い出して、夜中に飛び起きることがあります。本当は、戦争のことを忘れたいんです。でも、平和な世の中になるようにと考えると、できるだけ戦争の話をみんなに知らせたいとも思うのです。「どんなことがあっても、戦争だけはやってはならない」と言いたいです。それが私の一番の願いです。

●取材を終えて

仲里 昌晴 さん

正直なところ、私は戦争という言葉を聞いても、ドラマや映画で見るような戦争しか思い浮かびませんでした。単に、「怖いな」「かわいそうだな」といった思いしか持てていませんでした。

しかし今回、実際に戦争を体験した屋比

久さんのお話を聞いて、自分の考えていた戦争よりも、実際はとても生々しく、残酷なことを知りました。

当時の人々は、他人のことは考える暇がなく自分もいつ死ぬのかわからない状態で、生きる希望もない、という状況の中に生きていました。普段なら「他人のために」と思っている人たちでも、いざ戦争を目の当たりにしたら、そうなってしまう人たちも多いだろうと思いました。

「戦争で死んだら名誉である。死ぬのは怖くない」——当時そう思っていた中学生の屋比久さんの心境は、今の私たちには考えられないことだと思いました。

戦争がない今の日本、これからも戦争はあってはならない。そのためにできること

は、戦争の現実を伝えていくこと。今回のお話を、次の世代の人たちに伝えていこうと思いました。

与座 万里花 さん

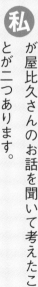

私が屋比久さんのお話を聞いて考えたことが二つあります。

一つ目は、残酷な過去はどれだけ時がたっても脳裏に焼きついて離れないということです。屋比久さんは私たちを気遣ってあまり悲惨な話はされなかったように感じました。それでも、言葉の端々から戦争の悲惨さや、考えるだけで怖いような当時の状況を想像することができました。

正直、私にとっては聞いているだけで、つ

らく、怖いことでした。ですから、実際に戦争を体験した屋比久さんがどんな思いをしてきたか、計り知れないと思います。「戦争は人を人じゃなくする」——学校で平和学習をしていた時の話が思い浮かびました。

でも、学校の先生も、戦争を体験したわけではありません。当事者である屋比久さんの言葉の一つ一つが貴重であり、私の心に強く残っています。

二つ目は、これから私たちがどう生きるかです。沖縄戦から七十年以上がたち、どんどん戦争体験者が少なくなっている現実があります。だからこそ、今を生きる私たちが大事だと考えました。

私は、今を生きる戦争を知らない世代、次の世代に「沖縄の心」を伝えることだと思い

ます。沖縄の心といっても、一人一人考え方は違うと思いますが、屋比久さんの話を聞いて、私が感じ取った沖縄の心。それは「真心」です。屋比久さんは当時、自分が生きることで精いっぱいであるにもかかわらず、周囲で人が亡くなる状況などを鮮明に覚えていました。無関心であれば周りの方々のことを思っていた屋比久さんの心がすごいはずです。私は、大変な中でも周りの方々のことを思っていた屋比久さんの心がすごいと思いました。

お話ししてくれた屋比久さんへの感謝を忘れず、感じ取ったことを次の世代につなげていきたいです。私のふるさと、沖縄で悲惨な戦争があったことを胸に刻み、日々の「当たり前」に感謝して生きていきます。

私の見た沖縄戦は「地獄の中の地獄」

▷証言者　比嘉 宗徳 さん
うるま市在住／84歳

▶取材者　宮里 徳人 さん
高校1年生

安里 杏珠 さん
中学2年生

岩﨑 将太 さん
中学1年生

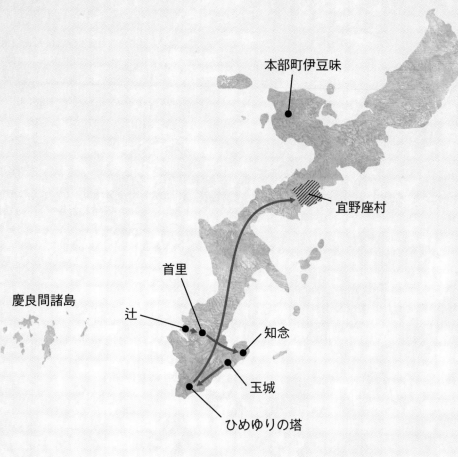

本部町伊豆味

宜野座村

首里

慶良間諸島

辻

知念

玉城

ひめゆりの塔

にぎやかだった戦前の那覇市

私の両親は沖縄出身ですが、大阪の紡績工場に勤めていたと聞いています。私の生まれが沖縄なのか大阪なのか、今となってはわかりません。戦争で家族を失ったため、私の生い立ちを教えてもらうことができません。物心ついた時は沖縄で生活していました。父は少尉だったと聞いていますが、随分前に亡くなって、父の顔もわかりません。

私の家族は那覇市の辻という町に暮らしていました。当時の辻は那覇の街の中心的な繁華街で、にぎやかでした。端道、中道、後道という大通りがあり、人力車がガジュマルの木陰のあちこちでお客を待っていました。ずらっと並んだ料亭はとても大きく立派なものでした。山形屋と円山号という大きなデパートもありました。那覇市役所の塔、町病院、大きな書店、大きい鳥居、芝居小屋、新垣バスという石炭を燃やして走るバス……、私が見ていた那覇はにぎやかで、すごかったです。

那覇市波之上から、港に向かっていったところにある、奥村渠という地域があり、私たち家族はにぎやかな町から少し離れたところにある、瓦屋根の家に住んでいました。一緒に暮らしていたのは、母と姉と妹、私の四人でしたが、その家には他の人たちも共同で暮らし

ていました。汗水節（あしみじぶし）という民謡で「一日に五十文（グンジュ＝一厘（りん））」と歌われているように、一日働いても少しの手間賃しかもらえなかったような人々が寄り集まって暮らしている感じでした。村はずれに三文殊（さんもうじ）と言って、鉄塔のようにそびえている大きい岩の塊（かたまり）があり、海も近かったです。目の前が波之上でした。小さな私は、浅いところで泳いでいました。辻の町を取り囲むように大きな墓がいくつもありました。こうした当時の那覇の町は、十月十日の空襲で燃えて全部灰になりました。

私は上山国民学校（うえのやま）に通っていました。学校へは母が縫（ぬ）った着物を着て通いました。帯を持っていなかったので、縄を巻いて登校していました。母なりに考えて、あり合わせのものを着させてくれていたのだと思います。靴もなく裸足でした。カバンも持っていないので、風呂敷にちょっとしたノートと鉛筆を包んで腰に巻いて行きました。鉛筆は、お姉さんたちが使って短くなった鉛筆に竹をさして、持つところを長くして使っていました。私たち家族は、何も捨てないで、ものを大事に使っていました。

私はウーマクー（わんぱく）でした。人の言うことを素直に聞こうとしないような子で、親の言うことも、誰の言うことも聞きません。ですから、学校では先生に叱（しか）られてばかりです。私は勉強もしないで、おしゃべりしたり、木に登ったり、悪さをしては校長室で叱

54

られていました。友達はいませんでした。貧乏人と言われ、嫌われていたんです。辻には大和（県外）からの寄留商人の子たちもいて、貧富の差がありました。商人の息子たちは洋服もちゃんとしていて、すごかったです。いじめもありました。そんな中で私は「男一匹」という感じでした。

那覇で見た「十・十空襲」

一九四四（昭和十九）年の十月十日に空襲がありました。当時は球部隊（牛島 満 中将率いる第三十二軍の通称）の兵隊さんたちが、岩場に陣地を造って、地上戦に備えていました。空からグラマン（戦闘機）が突っ込んできます。そこでパンパンと撃って反撃するのですが、撃っても撃っても飛行機は次々と飛んでくるんです。日本軍は限られた弾しかないと聞いていたので、見るからに太刀打ちできていない状態でした。

私たち家族は「十・十空襲」の後、追われるように母の故郷の本島北部の本部町 伊豆味に行きました。私は母におぶわれての移動でした。一度は実家へ疎開したものの、母は何を考えたのか、子どもを連れてすぐに那覇に戻っていました。しばらくは空襲もなく戦争が来るとは思ってもいませんでした。

辻にはたくさんの亀甲墓（かめこうばか）があります。沖縄の墓は大きいですから、その墓を利用して、兵隊たちが寝る場所を作ってくれました。お墓の中にある遺骨の入った甕（かめ）は外に出して、焼け残ったトタンなどを利用していました。周りは焼け野原だったので、墓の中はまだ良いほうでした。

古い墓は日本軍の基地でした。目の前は那覇港がよく見渡せ、格好の場所だったと思います。母は兵隊さんのご飯作りに専念していました。その残りを子どもに食べさせて、養っていたのだと思います。

米軍の空襲、攻撃が激しくなっていきました。特に那覇港はすごかったです。私の家のすぐ目の前でした。慶良間（けらま）（諸島）のほうから艦砲射撃がポンポンポンポンと那覇港に撃ち込まれ、グラマンが連隊を組んで飛んできます。私はその様子を、怖いというのではなく、何か面白いという感じで見ていました。ものすごい光景でした。あちらの米軍もたくさん弾を撃ち、こちらの日本軍も撃ち返すんです。お互い、すごく激しい。日本軍は、機関砲を墓の中に入れていました。二十から三十人兵隊がいたと思います。

戦後に聞いた話ですが、本当に優秀な人は武部隊（たけ）といって、台湾あたりに行っていたそうです。沖縄本島に置かれていた兵隊は、あまり力のない兵隊だということでした。

一瞬で「消えた」家族

ある日、「米軍がまもなく上陸するから、みんな逃げなさい」と命令が出たんです。軍刀を持っている兵隊でした。とうとう戦争が来るんだと思いました。私たちは母の判断で逃げることにし、首里のほうへ向かいました。首里は軍の司令部があるところです。母と姉と妹と私の四人で逃げました。

艦砲射撃は激しく、上からも下からも、ものすごい火力で攻撃されました。どうして良いか、わからないんです。辛抱できずに動こうものなら、機関銃を撃ち込まれます。知念・玉城までは家族四人一緒でした。

ある日の昼間です。食べ物を探して帰ってくると、隠れていたところに爆弾が落とされて、兵隊も民間人もいっぺんに目の前からいなくなっていました。どこを探しても私の母、姉、妹がいないのです。さっきまで一緒だったのに、いなくなっていました。そこでわかりました。「ああ、母は亡くなったんだな」。その気持ちは今でも言い表せるものではありません。涙も出なかったです。ただ、ぽかんとしていました。それからは、一人ぼっちで

す。私の家族は戦争で殺されました。

「怖い」という気持ちはなかったです。全然怖くない。そのころには私の魂はもう死んでいたのかもしれません。多くの人が目の前で殺されました。でも、不思議なことに、自分には弾が当たらないんです。私は背も小さかったから、その点は良かったのかもしれません。

戦場では、地面にお腹をくっつけて、ワニのように歩いていました。目の前で多くの人が無残にも死んでいくのを見て、自分なりに身を守る方法を考えて逃げました。もしも私が正々堂々と歩いていたら、とっくに殺されていたでしょう。

一人になっても私は逃げ続けました。なんでも食べました。なんでもやらないと生き延びることはできません。だから、人のやらないこともやりました。

一人戦場をさまよう

日が沈んで暗くなったら、照明弾が飛びます。照明弾が上がると、夜が明けたように明るくなります。すぐにどこかに潜らないといけません。潜るといっても、穴などありませんから、芋畑のカズラの上や、さとうきび畑に突っ込む感じで隠れるのです。

どこが安全だとか、今逃げろとか言う人など誰もいないので、自分で自分の命を守るた

めに必死でした。米軍に捕まったら、命はないというのが頭にありました。飛び込んだ畑には、ヘビやネズミなど、いろんな動物もウロウロしています。私はそれを捕まえて食べました。誰に笑われようと構わなかったです。笑う人もいなかったと思いますが。

私が隠れていたところに友軍がやってきて、「あっちに行きなさい」「出ていけ」と言うんです。言うことを素直に聞かないとすぐ殺されてしまいます。子どもも大人も関係ありませんでした。隠れるのにいい場所はほとんど日本軍に取られていました。私は言われる通りにその場所を立ち退きました。すると、一、二分後にはその場所が爆撃されたということもありました。運がいい、悪いということが、生きることを左右していました。

今の「ひめゆりの塔」（糸満市伊原）へも逃げました。戦闘はそこが一番激しかったです。米軍も友軍も沖縄の人もごっちゃになって、たくさんの人たちが亡くなっていました。逃げようとしたら、バラバラバラと機関銃で撃たれます。どこからともなく弾が飛んできます。そのころは壕（ごう）というものもなく、さとうきびの枯れた葉っぱを原野に立てかけて、そこに隠れているような状態でした。上からも下からも攻撃されています。爆弾が破裂したら人間も粉々になります。近くに爆弾が落ち、爆風で飛んできた土に埋まりました。土の重さがのしかかってい

したが、その土を自分で払いのけると、今度は海のほうへ向かって逃げました。さとうきび畑に隠れて、さとうきびをかじりながら必死に生き延びていました。ガタガタガタと聞きなれない音に振り返ると、そこには米軍の戦車が迫っていました。見たこともない車でした。

米軍は、民間人も兵隊もさとうきび畑に潜んで隠れているのをわかっているようでした。日本語で「戦争は終わった。出てきなさい」と言っていました。だけど捕まったら殺されると思っていたので、私は決して出ませんでした。

米軍は投降してこないと、火炎放射器でサーッと焼き殺すのです。目の前のさとうきび畑が燃えさかります。あっちに逃げる人、こっちに逃げる人、その場で焼け死んでいく人もいました。

私は逃げました。大人が十五人ほどいる壕に潜りこみました。何も言うことなく潜りこんだのですが、大人にばれて、首をつかまれて外に投げられました。子どもがいると足手まといだからでしょう。「どこかへ行け」と言われても、行くところもないのです。その場にだまって立っていました。壕には入れてもらえない、しかし、あまりにも戦闘が激しいので、外にいるよりはと無理やりに入っていきました。生きるためには、もうどうなっ

60

てもいいという気持ちでした。

残酷で凄惨な戦争の現実

　戦場では、頭がおかしくなる人もいました。

　ある日本兵は軍服を脱ぎ捨てて、亡くなっている沖縄のおじいさんの着物をはぎ取り身につけ、民間人に偽装していました。しかし兵隊ですから、いざという時に備えて、銃と手榴弾は持っているのです。降伏する気はないのだろうと感じていました。壕で日本兵は、「ここから一歩も出るな。出たらやる（殺す）」と言い出しました。恐ろしくなってみんなでじっとしていましたが、緊迫した状況に耐えられなくなった人がいて、逃げようとして拳銃で撃たれました。私の目の前です。手も足も出ないです。助けるとか、どうしようもできないです。その亡くなった人を一週間くらいは壕に置いていました。

　戦場では数多くの人が亡くなっているというのに、全く臭くなかったです。そうでなくても風呂にも入らず、汚れているので臭いのは当然のことですが、どういうわけか臭いを感じませんでした。感覚が麻痺していたのだと思います。

　ヘビとか、ムカデは棒で捕って食べました。芋畑には種芋が植えられているので、その

芋を取って食べていました。一番のご馳走はカエルでした。腿のところをちぎって、全部生で食べていました。

おしっこも飲みました。錆びついた缶を拾ってきて、ゆすぎもしないで、おしっこをためて飲むのです。ひもじいという感覚もなくなり、「いつ死ぬのか」という恐怖を抱いているだけでした。戦場では死んだ人のポケットを片っ端から探りました。ポケットには砂糖やカンパンがありました。それを食べて過ごしたのです。

たくさん飢え死にしている子どもたちを見ました。お母さんは死んでも、子どもは生きているんです。私たちはそれを助けることができないのです。助けようとすれば、自分もやられるんですから。泥棒もしました。

壕の中で、沖縄の住民たちが、寝ている友軍の首を絞めて殺すところも見ました。住民を脅迫する友軍は、命を脅かす恐怖の存在でした。住民たちは生きていくために、そのような行動に出ました。何が何やらわからない時間を過ごしていました。

学校の先生と生徒らしき人たちが、手榴弾で自決しようとする場面にも遭遇しました。その人たちは手榴弾のピンを抜いたものの、信管が働かず不発でした。

戦後、沖縄戦の映像を見る機会がありますが、私の経験はあの映像とは全然違います。

私が体験した沖縄戦はもっと残酷で凄惨なものでした。

逃げ続け、生き延びた果てに

私は「どんなことがあっても逃げる」と決めていました。

アメリカ兵の寝泊まりする陣地にも入りました。同じくらいの年ごろの子どもたち数人で入り、米軍のトラックに乗り込みました。車は収容所で停まりました。親のいない戦争孤児が集められているようでした。子どもたちが何十人もいて、女も男も裸で下着もはかされずにいる姿を見て、ここでは捕まりたくないと思いました。ところが私たち四人は見つかってしまい、捕まりました。私は諦めずに、米兵の巡回の隙を突いてフェンスの下に潜って、お腹を擦りながら一人で逃げました。

一人ぼっちになって行くあてもありません。そのころは、逃げ続けることに疲れ果てて「母の故郷へ行こう」という気持ちになっていました。ただ十歳の私の足では本島北部の本部町はあまりにも遠く、そこまで行くことは困難でした。

多くの避難民が収容されている本島北部の宜野座村まで逃げた時、かやぶき家が造られ、その中に避難民がいっぱいいるのを見ました。それで、米軍は住民を殺さないことがだん

だんとわかってきていました。心のどこかで、私のことも助けてほしいと願うようになっていました。この先をなんとかして生きていかなければならないと、幼心に思っていたのです。

ろくに食事もせず、川の水を飲んで過ごしていました。栄養失調状態でお腹も出ていました。私は米兵の上着をジャンパーみたいに羽織って、ズボンは履いていませんでした。ズボンがなくても、ジャンパーで足のところまで隠れるので問題ありません。

宜野座の農家の庭先で、たくさん芋が炊かれているのを見つけました。私はその芋を食べながら、上着のポケットに芋を突っ込んでいました。お腹いっぱいになったと思った時、近くの人に見つかってしまいました。

「帰れ」と言われ、棒で殴られました。でも、私は疲れて、もう逃げたくありませんでした、帰る場所もないのです。

しばらくして、一人ぼっちの私の素性がわかったのでしょうか、農家の主人は追い払うのをやめ、私をこの家に置いてくれると言い出しました。「働いてくれたら、みんなと同じように育ててあげるよ、頑張ろうね」と言われました。畑の労働力として置いてくれたのかもしれません。行き場のない私は、それでいいと思い、この家で働くことにしたので

64

す。

この家の母さんには、すごく可愛がられました。家族の中で暮らすようになってから、私は人間らしく変わっていきました。だんだんと感情が戻ってきて、魂が生き返ったような気がしました。もちろんその家族は私の命の恩人です。今も盆・正月はずっと通っています。宜野座村松田の安村さんという方でした。

戦後は、石川の消防署に三十年勤めました。天涯孤独と思っていた私も、素晴らしい奥さんにも巡りあえ、私の生活は一変しました。今では二人の息子と七人の孫に囲まれています。百歳まで生きるというのが私の目標です。

私は人の経験したことのないことを経験しました。運があって、なんとか生きしのいできたと思います。戦争孤児として逃げて、生きてきました。そこまでしてなぜ生きようと思ったのかは、今でもわかりません。ただ必死で生きていただけ、本能なのかもしれません。そして、地獄の中の地獄を経験したからこそ、戦争には何があっても反対なのです。

● 取材を終えて

宮里 徳人 さん

（二）

二〇一九年三月二十三日、比嘉さんは僕たち中高生三人に自分の戦争体験を話してくださいました。比嘉さんは「戦争は極限状態で、私の心は死んでいた」とおっしゃいました。親、きょうだいも亡くなり、友達もいなくて孤独にただ生きるために逃げていた比嘉さんは、本当にすごい人だと思いました。

もし僕が比嘉さんの立場になったとしたら、僕は親、きょうだい、友達、知り合いもいない中で生きる意味を見失ってしまい、生きることを諦めていただろうと思います。比嘉さんの話を聞いて、これから先の時代に、絶対に戦争は起こしてはならないと

思いました。戦争は何も生み出しません。負けたほうはもちろん勝ったほうも、どちらも得をしません。それなのに戦争をする人間は、愚かだと思いました。戦争は、絶対に忘れてはいけない歴史の一ページだと僕は考えます。

安里 杏珠 さん

㊙私

は、比嘉宗徳さんから沖縄戦の話を聞いて、一番初めに頭に浮かんだ言葉は、「過酷」でした。そう思った理由は三つあります。

まず一つ目は、環境の変化です。なぜなら、十歳まで平凡で幸せな生活を送っていたのに、いきなり戦争が始まって、住んでいた場

所が戦場となったと話していたからです。

二つ目は、食べ物です。戦争は食べ物が少なくなるというのは知っていましたが、カエルや虫を食べて生き延びたということは知りませんでした。

最後は「魂が死んでいた」という言葉です。

私が「一番つらかったことは何ですか？」と質問した際に、「何もない。なぜかと言うとね、魂が死んでいるから家族が死んでも泣かなかったし、死体を見てもなんとも思わなかった」と答えられ、戦争は人の心までも奪ってしまうのだと思いました。

戦争はしてはいけないし、二度と起こさないためにも、私たちの世代が後世にこの過酷な戦争の姿を、語り継いでいきます。

岩﨑 将太 さん

㋑ は、戦争について、周りの人と同じようにテレビで見たり授業で学んだりして、ある程度のことは理解しているつもりでした。しかし今回のように、一人の方からじっくりと話を聞くことで、より深く戦争体験者の気持ちを知ることができました。

比嘉さんから「感情がなくなり、目の前で人が死んでも怖いとも思わなかった」と聞き、私はとても驚きました。戦争という、いつ死ぬかもわからない状況では、人は普通の精神状態ではなくなるのだと思いました。

話を聞くだけでも怖いのに、実際に戦争になったらどうなるのだろうと思いました。大切な人を失ったり……戦

争は絶対にあってはならないと思います。でも、戦争の真実がこの先、世の中に知られなくなっていったとしたら、いつかまた戦争が起きるかもしれません。だから、こうして学んだからには、戦争の恐ろしさを忘れずに、風化させないように伝え広めて、戦争をこの世からなくしたいです。

報われずに死んだ
兄への思い

▷証言者　仲村 傳さん
　　　　　　（なかむら　でん）
島尻郡与那原町在住／88歳

▶取材者　伊敷 裕さん
　　　　　　（いしき　ゆたか）
高校2年生

黒木 裕子さん
（くろき　ゆうこ）
中学2年生

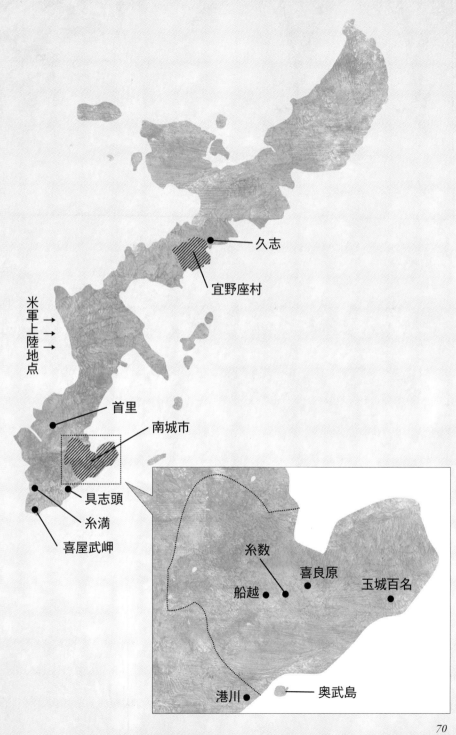

久志

宜野座村

米軍上陸地点 → → →

首里

南城市

具志頭

糸満

喜屋武岬

糸数

船越

喜良原

玉城百名

港川

奥武島

働き者で優秀だった兄

私が国民学校高等一年の十三歳の時に、沖縄戦がありました。私たちの世代は、生まれた一九三一（昭和六）年に満州事変があり、中国との戦争が始まりました。「十五年戦争」は、第二次世界大戦が終わるまでのことです。景気も悪く、あまりいい時代じゃなかったと思います。

そのころは、十四歳以上の男子は防衛隊、義勇隊に召集されていました。私のすぐ上の兄は三歳上で、十六歳でした。義勇隊に取られて、特攻隊になりました。戦争の話をする時に、一番つらいのは兄のことを思い出すことです。

私たち家族は沖縄本島の南部、旧玉城村玉城一区（現・南城市玉城百名）、玉城城の城下に暮らしていました。百名の海は遠浅で、美しい青い海でした。私はそこで泳いで遊んでいました。一番上に兄・傳進。次が十三歳の私。後は小さい子どもたちでした。母は目が悪く、遠くのものは見えませんでしたが、身の回りのことはできました。小さいころに首里に奉公に行っていたので、言葉づかいが丁寧でした。沖縄風のカンプー（束ねた髪形）を結い、着物をつけていました。わが家は父がおらず、兄が働いて母を助けていました。

兄は学校へ通いながら、働いて、私たちにご飯を食べさせてくれていました。それなのに、戦争に行かされ、死んでしまったのです。戦争の話をするたびにこのことを思い出して、涙がこぼれます。青春時代がなかった兄が不憫でたまらないのです。兄は私たちの犠牲になったとも言えるのです。

兄は村一番の働き者と言われていたそうです。本人は苦しくて、「大変に難儀だ」と漏らしたことがありました。私はその時五、六年生になっていました。六年生くらいからは、私も兄の手伝いをしていました。

村一番の働き者、優秀と言われても、戦争で亡くなるなんて……。生きている時も苦労しているのに、戦争にもやられて、時々はそんな兄を思い出して、夜寝ていても、涙がこぼれます。

この思いがあるので、戦争体験の話をすることは、なるべく避けるようになっていました。

艦砲射撃の恐怖

一九四四（昭和十九）年ごろからは、私の通う国民学校に軍隊が来て、学校は全部占領

され、軍隊の宿泊場所になっていました。私たちは、地域の字事務所で勉強していましたが、そこへも軍隊が入るようになって、結局ほとんど勉強はできませんでした。一日中作業に駆り出されていたのです。ほどなく兄は召集されていきました。

一九四五（昭和二十）年三月二十三日はちょうど彼岸でした。わが家では彼岸のためにもち米を炊いていました。

空襲警報が鳴り、飛行機がブンブンと飛んできます。家に残っているきょうだいの中では私が一番上でした。私は自分の身支度を整えると、家畜の綱を切り、逃がしました。そうこうしているうちに焼夷弾が飛んできて、かやぶき屋根に火がつきました。自分では消すこともできず、どうしようもできない状態でした。わが家は村でも最初に焼かれてしまいました。その中を自分たちは這うように、避難壕に逃げたのです。

翌日からは艦砲射撃です。空襲で家も焼けてなくなり、壕の生活が始まりました。家が残った人たちも、戦闘が激しくて家には帰れませんでした。どの壕に避難するのかは決まっていて、私たち家族はワチバルの壕に避難しました。しばらくして、ここが危ないということで、タチアブ（字仲村渠二区）というところの壕に移動しました。ハシゴをかけて下りていくような壕でした。

どれくらい艦砲射撃が撃ち込まれたでしょうか。艦砲射撃の激しさを表す言葉で「艦砲ぬ喰えーぬくさー（艦砲射撃の食い残し）」と言っていました。沖縄中が艦砲射撃で砲弾を浴びて多くの人が死に、生き残った人は弾の食い残しのようなものだということです。艦砲射撃で大きな爆弾が落ちると、地面がえぐられて、着弾痕は直径十メートル近くの穴ができます。雨が降ったら、そこに水が溜まってプールみたいになるほどでした。

玉城の高台、喜良原には日本軍の陣地がありました。米軍が本島南部の港川から上陸するという噂があり、玉城糸数の大砲は、全て港川や奥武島へ向けられていました。私もその大砲を向ける作業を手伝いに行きました。ところが、米軍は南部からは上陸しませんでした。本島南部の奥武島へ戦車を下ろす真似をして、そこからぐるりと回って、本島中部の西海岸、北谷、読谷から上陸したのです。米軍は沖縄を二分して、片方は南の島尻へ、もう片方は北部へ向けて進軍しました。

壕での避難生活の最中、艦砲射撃があっても、作業をしないといけません。「陣地作業に出ろ」と言われても、皆、爆弾の炸裂が恐ろしくて、作業に行くことができません。恐れをなす避難民に対して、日本兵が「（命令を）聞かないものは！」と軍刀を抜きました。女性、子ども、年寄りも恐ろしい思いをしながら陣地作業に行きました。雨のように降り

注ぐ艦砲射撃の中、陣地や避難壕掘りの作業をさせられていました。

地下壕での避難生活

今のゴルフ場がある玉城の喜良原には大きな地下壕があり、その自然壕は首里から南下した負傷兵たちで溢れ返っていました。私は負傷兵の看護を手伝いに行きました。壕の中はジメジメとして蒸し風呂のようです。苦しそうなうめき声で地獄でした。胸を撃ち抜かれて苦しんでいる負傷兵を団扇であおぎ、医者や看護師の手当てを待っていました。そのうちに負傷兵の胸からブクブクと血が溢れだし、見ている私は血の気が引いて卒倒しました。

暗い壕の中ではいつ夜が明けたのかわかりません。トイレも壕の中ですませていました。外に出ないので、いつの間にか日付感覚もなくなり、このころの記憶はあいまいで、ぽっかりと空白になってしまっています。

五月下旬には、与那原から米軍が上がってきました。雨が降り注いでいました。壕の入り口まで米兵が来て「出なさい」と言うのです。私たちは捕虜になって恥をかくより死んだほうがいいと教育され、出たら殺されると教えられているので誰も動きません。ところ

が、数人が手を上げて出ていったのです。

私はそれを隠れて見ていました。するとそこに私の父の姿があったのです。父は母と別れて別に所帯を持っていたので、同じ壕にいても、私たちと一緒にいることはありませんでした。

戦争が終わった後に、「なぜ壕を出る時に一緒に出ようと言ってくれなかったのか」と父に尋ねたことがあります。父は「捕虜は殺さないはずだから手を上げて出なさい」と聞かされていたと言います。しかし、壕の中でそれを口にすると、家族全員がスパイの疑いをかけられて、殺されてしまう恐れがあったのです（当時は夜勝手に出歩いたり、沖縄の言葉を使うだけで日本軍から殺されてしまうこともありました）。壕には日本兵がいましたので、何も話すことができなかったとのことでした。

捕虜になっても殺されないということがわかっていれば、私たちも一緒に出ていったでしょう。それを知らずにいたので、壕の奥のほうへ逃げ隠れ、戦場を逃げ回って悲惨な目にあうこととなったのです。

夜になると、何組かの家族が荷物を背負って壕を出ていきました。私たち家族も、母と私と妹（十歳）、弟（七歳）、いとこの五人で壕を出て、雨の中を南部に向かって逃げました。

76

行くあてもなく逃げ惑う日々

母は頭に荷物を載せ、私も食料などの袋を持ち、その後を歩きました。目の悪い母が一緒なので、子どもが歩くほどの速度でした。ごろごろと死体が転がる道を逃げました。土砂降りの中を泥まみれになりながら、道端に伏せながら歩き続けました。

「ババーン」と砲弾の炸裂音がすると、頭や肩に爆風で飛ばされた土がパラパラパラと降りかかります。それが弾の破片だったらおしまいです。命を落とします。爆発があるとしばらくは、頭がボーッとします。何秒間か意識がない状態から、ハッとわれに返り、一緒にいる家族のことを思い出して、名前を呼んで、はぐれないように手を取って走ります。

十三歳の私が家族を率いていました。行くあてもなく、人がいるから後を追って歩くという避難の仕方でした。

四、五人のグループで畑に食べ物を取りに行き、地雷に気がついたということもありました。日本軍が地雷を埋めた場所は、人が入らないので野菜が豊富にありました。地雷を避けてキャベツを取ったり、にんじんを取ったりしました。今考えてもヒヤヒヤします。何回も危険な目にあい、いつやられてもおかしくなよく生きていたものだなと思います。

い場面がありました。

逃げる途中、弟の腿に流れ弾の破片が当たり、負傷しました。傷口をタオルで縛り、母がおぶって、安全な壕を探しました。土手に造られた防空壕を見つけ、そこに潜りこみました。隣の壕にも家族づれが隠れていて、子どもの声がしていました。しばらくして、迫撃砲による攻撃が始まりました。迫撃砲は溝を掘ったように、一列に並んで撃たれるので大変に危険です。大砲が機関銃のように来ます。赤ちゃんの声が聞こえた隣の壕は、全滅でした。ここも危ないと感じ、夜には出ました。

私たちのような子どものいる家族は、他の避難民からも疎まれました。やっとのことで安全な壕を探して入ると、壕には避難民や日本兵がいました。その時、「ドカン」という音がして、日本兵が「声を出すな、子どもを泣かすな」と言っていたのを覚えています。壕の入り口に弾を撃ち込まれると、きつい臭いがしました。毒ガスだと思い鼻と口に布をあて、喉の痛みと息苦しさにじっと耐えました。

夜には壕を脱出しましたが、右往左往しているだけで、どこへ逃げたらいいのかわからず、兵隊に聞きました。「日本軍は喜屋武岬へ向かう」「住民は糸満のほうへ行きなさい」と言われ、歩きました。最後は家族だけになっていました。

米軍の影に怯えて

月夜の晩でした。突然、人影が見えました。私の目の前にアメリカ兵が突っ立っていたのです。私は恐ろしくなり、食料を投げ捨て、茂みに隠れました。しかしよく見ると、月に照らされ長く伸びた米兵の影で、目の前に現れたわけではありませんでした。命の危機に直面して神経はすり減り、少しのことにも敏感になっていたのです。

食料を全部捨ててしまって水もありません。何も食べていないので、そこらへんの木の葉もむしって食べました。

月夜に壕を這い出して、崖を下りました。しばらくすると、機関銃射撃にあいました。知らずに敵陣に入り込んでしまっていたのです。走って逃げる途中に、母の足指に銃弾が当たりました。私は「動くなよ、伏せて、動くな!」と家族に叫びました。逃げる時は私が全部指示していました。全員そのままじっとしていました。

朝方に、這うようにしてさとうきび畑まで行き、さとうきびを家族でかじりました。もう、何もないのです。その時に、赤鬼みたいな大きな体の米兵に銃を向けられました。もう降参です。私はもう頭が真っ白になって、何が何やらわかりません。米兵の言っている

こともわからず、こちらの言葉も通じません。米兵が帰れと言っているようだったので、母のところに戻りました。その後、私たち家族は両手を上げ捕虜になりました。不思議と全員生き残っていました。

傷だらけの家族を守りながら

　負傷した弟の傷口からは、うじ虫がわいていました。私のおしっこをかけて消毒していましたが、もう少しで破傷風になる重症でした。母も負傷していたので、私たち家族は糸満から軍病院のある本島北部の宜野座の収容所へ移動させられました。

　宜野座は食糧難でした。避難民がいっぱいで食糧はありません。田んぼを歩きまわって、カエルなどタンパク質はないか探しました。しかし、カエルもいないのです。カズラの葉っぱさえないのです。わずかな配給米を食べてしのいでいました。長姉は本島北部の山原に避難していましたが、食べ物もない状態で、おっぱいが出ず、栄養失調で子どもを亡くしていました。

　久志（現在の名護市）というところにチリ焼き場がありました。ここには米軍が不要なものを捨てていました。トラックが来てチリを捨てると、私のような少年たちは、一目散に

走って出ていき、食べ物を探します。時には大きな牛缶を見つけ「戦果だ!」と言って喜んで持ち帰り、なんとか飢えをしのいでいました。

私は中学生でしたが、おにぎり一個をもらうために茅刈り作業に行き、家族で分けて食べていました。そのころは、兄は戦争に行ったままで、生きているか死んだかもわかりませんでした。兄の消息がわかったのは、地元に戻ってからでした。

兄は戦死していました。小学生の五、六年から親や弟妹を食べさせるために、これ以上働けないというくらい、懸命に働いてきた兄。それなのに十六歳という若さで、何も報われることなく、戦争によって無残な死を遂げたと思うと、たまらないのです。私は兄を思い出すと泣きたくなるんです。苦労した兄には、幸福になってほしかった。戦争のために死んでしまったことが、残念でならないのです。

私は兄の同級生と一緒に遺骨を探しに行きました。具志頭(現・八重瀬町)で遺骨を見つけ、お墓に収めることができました。私は義兄四人を戦争で失っていますが、多くはどこで命を落としたのか、わからないです。

逃げることは悪いことではない

一九四六（昭和二十一）年までに玉城に帰りました。最初に帰ったところは玉城の船越の仮小屋でした。生まれ育った字玉城一区は米軍基地化されて帰れず、仮小屋生活が続きました。その後も村内で移転を繰り返しました。

玉城初等学校を卒業したのは一九四七（昭和二十二）年でした。戦争で高等二年を終了していないので、戦後にもう一度高等二年をやり直しました。さらに教育制度が六三三制に変わったことで、高校は卒業まで四年かかりました。当時は米軍の払い下げのHBTと呼ばれる服を着ていることが多かったです。服の後ろにはCIV（民間人）やPW（捕虜）とペンキで書かれていました。私はCIVと書かれた洋服を着ていました。ノートもないので紙切れをぐるぐる巻いたものを使っていました。

戦争で沖縄の優秀な人材が亡くなりました。中学、師範学校の生徒は将来教師になる予定の人たちでした。戦争に駆り出されて多くの命が奪われ、戦後は教師がいませんでした。教員の不足から、高卒の私も学校現場へ推薦されたのです。学校で働きながら、糸満訓練学校で半年学び、夏休みのたびに講習を受けて、教員になりました。そのころから生活は

やっと安定していきました。その後は沖縄を平和で豊かな郷土にしようと、教育者として歩んできました。

戦場では、逃げるのに精いっぱい、食べるのに精いっぱいでした。家族をどう守るかに懸命でした。嫌だなということからは逃げることしか考えなかったです。だから私は生き残ったと思うのです。逃げることは悪いことではありません。時には、誰の言うことにも従わずに、自分の命を守ることが必要なのです。親の言いつけに背いて、死んだふりをして、集団自決から逃げた人もいたと聞きます。生きる力を培っていくのが、教育の大事なところです。沖縄には「命どぅ宝」という言葉があります。命が大事なのです。どんなことがあっても、戦争はやってはいけない。戦争は勝っても負けても、命が犠牲になることに変わりはないのです。

伊敷 裕 さん

仲 村さんの戦争体験を聞いて、戦争はもう二度と起こしてはいけないということを今一度、強く思い知らされました。なぜなら、仲村さんはこの戦争で自分たちのために一生懸命に働いてくれた、大切な家族であるお兄さんを亡くしました。今でも戦争の話になるとお兄さんのことを思い出し、泣きたくなると聞きました。

僕は、家族はもちろん、大切な人やお世話になった人を失った経験はありません。こんな僕でも突然目の前から大切な人がいなくなり、もう二度と会うことができなくなったとしたら、とても言葉に表すことができないほどの喪失感や絶望感に打ちひし

がれることは、簡単に想像できます。

さらに、そんな状況なのに仲村さんは、日付や時間もわからない中、いつ襲ってくるかもしれない、雨のように降る爆弾の中を逃げ続けたと聞きました。僕には想像すらできないくらい恐ろしく、つらいことだと思います。

最後に、仲村さんは「自分を顧みなさい。どんなにつらいことがあったとしても、自分を大切にしなさい」ということを僕たちに言ってくれました。僕はこの言葉が一番心に残っています。きっと大人になっても忘れず、いつまでも胸にしっかりと残っていると思うし、残していきたいです。

今回このような体験を聞く機会を作っていただき、また、つらい体験にもかかわらず

語っていただいた仲村さんには感謝しています。

大切な人や多くの命を奪い、悲しくつらい思いしか残らない戦争、勝っても負けてもどちらにも犠牲が生まれる戦争。こんな戦争はもう二度と起こしてはならないことだと深く心に刻み込みました。

黒木 裕子 さん

㊙は、あらためて戦争の恐ろしさを知りました。

今まで、私は、家族がいつもそばにいてくれるというのは、当たり前のことのように思っていました。でも、戦争というのは、大切な家族を、そして自分という人間を死と

いう恐怖へ突き落とすことだと知りました。

しかし、この沖縄の地で、「鉄の暴風」と呼ばれるほど激しい戦争があり、死というものが身近にあったということは想像が難しいですし、実感もわきません。

今の平和な沖縄から、平和ではなかった当時の沖縄を想像できる人は少ないと思います。

私も考えたことがありませんでした。今回、「平和とは何か」ということについて、深く考えさせられました。

平和という言葉の裏に隠されているもの、平和を支えているものは何なのでしょうか。

それは、仲村さんが言っていたように「命（ぬち）どぅ宝」ではないのかと、今、私は思います。

仲村さんは、「どんなことがあっても戦争

を起こしてはならない。戦いには勝っても負けても民が犠牲になるよ」と言っていました。体験者のメッセージ、バトンを私たち

が受け取り、次の世代へつないでいこうと思います。

戦争が終わっても、苦しみは消えない

▷証言者　與古田 光順 さん
宜野湾市在住／84歳

▶取材者　仲宗根 美幸 さん
高校2年生

南風原 宏明 さん
中学2年生

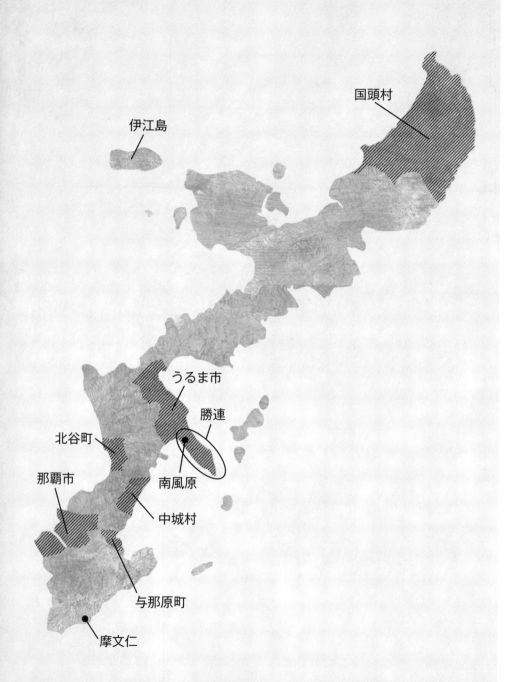

国頭村

伊江島

うるま市

勝連

北谷町

那覇市

南風原

中城村

与那原町

摩文仁

戦前の思い出

私は自分の命を絶っていたかもしれないくらいの被害を、この戦争から受けたんです。

仕事中でも緊張するとおしっこが漏れて流れます。それは無意識のうちにです。座っているところ、着ている服、所構わず汚してしまいます。その次には、便が二十日も出なくなる極度な便秘を起こします。頭もおかしくなってしまいそうになります。

戦争はだめだという気持ちを忘れないために、このような難病にかかったのではと思うこともあります。

私たち家族は、戦争が始まる前は、旧那覇の西新町（現・那覇市西町）に暮らしていました。にぎやかな繁華街で、真楽座という芝居小屋の隣で祖母が雑貨店を経営していました。

真楽座の劇団は非常に人気で、芝居見物の客がひっきりなしに、くんぺんやタンナファクルーという菓子や飲み物を買ってくれ、店は繁盛していました。私は朝起きると劇場の前を掃き掃除し、母の手伝いをよくしました。軽便鉄道に乗って与那原まで行き、農家からさとうきびを買い付けたりしたことも思い出します。

上山国民学校に通っていました。長兄は出征し、戦後に復員しました。戦争が始まる前

に、次男の兄と妹たちは母の実家の中城（なかぐすく）へと疎開（そかい）しました。いつしか家の二階に四、五人の通信兵が住むようになり、町に朝鮮人軍夫が増えてきているのを子どもながらに感じていました。芝居小屋が慰安所（いあんじょ）になり、たくさんの兵隊が並んでいました。

恐怖の空襲

　一九四四（昭和十九）年十月十日、まだ夜が明ける前に「バンバン」という音で目がさめました。その後、朝ご飯を食べていると空襲が始まりました。「十・十空襲」です。私はお箸（はし）を握ったまま、恐怖に怯（おび）えていました。

　警防団や班長が「逃げなさい！」「前もって決められたお墓に入りなさい」と声をかけています。朝の七時過ぎに、祖父と母、私と妹の恵子の四人で近くのお墓へ逃げ込みました。真楽座の裏に防空壕（ごう）になっているお墓がありました。歩いて五分くらい、走るとほんの二、三分のところです。　私の入ったお墓はすごく大きかったのですが、三十から四十人も入ると、足の踏み場もないくらいでした。　壕への避難は前もって演習をさせられていて、定員も決まっていたと思います。

逃げたのはいいのですが、私はおしっこがしたくなってきたんです。おしっこを外に出してくれと言いましたが、「今、君が外へ出ると、上から見られて、爆弾を落とされて他の人まで全滅する」と警防団員に言われました。私は我慢するしかないと、おしっこをこらえました。

爆撃の音は激しく、戦火がお墓の入り口まで来ていました。人が溢れんばかりの場所に、投げ込まれているような状態です。人の熱と炎の熱とで私は半ば死んでいるような状態でした。こうやって死ぬんだなと気が遠のくのを感じました。

ようやく飛行機が飛び去っていき、壕から出てもいいということになりました。夜の七時ごろと思いますが、私はほっとしました。真楽座も、十・十空襲により焼失しました。

その年に祖父が建てた二基の立派な亀甲墓（かめこうばか）も空襲にやられました。戦後、その墓地の土地は米軍基地に取られて、今はもうどこにあったのかもわからない状態です。

私たち家族は十・十空襲に追われて、その日の夜に那覇を出たのです。祖父の引率（いんそつ）で、母と私と妹の四人で一列になって歩きました。はだしで十四時間歩き続け、勝連の南風原（はえばる）（現・うるま市）へようやくたどり着きました。そこは祖母の実家があるところで、病弱な祖母は早めに疎開していたのです。

母は祖母に私を預けると、幼い妹を連れて出かけていきました。妹は三歳でした。父のところは親戚も多く安全でしたが、中城の母の実家は助ける人が誰もいないと心配をしていました。実家に預けた子どもたちや祖母を守るのは自分しかいないと、中城へ向かったのです。母が勝連にいたのは一日だけでした。

守りたかった命、全てを失った母

十・十空襲の時、父は伊江島（いえじま）のソテツ工場で軍属として働いていました。戦争中はソテツからデンプンをとり、航空燃料にしていました。その工場が伊江島にあり、軍の命令で徴用された人が働いていました。

家族は祖父を中心に勝連に疎開したとはいえ、子どもたちを抱えての生活は不安だったのでしょう。祖父は父へ何か知恵を使って帰ってきてくれないかと連絡をしました。父は勝連のみんなのいる家に戻ってきました。

祖母が体が弱く介護をしないといけないと理由をつけて、父と一緒に母と弟妹たちが帰ってくるのを期待して、疎開先で待っていました。一方、子どもたちを迎えに行った母は、しばらくして家族を連れて中城からうるま市に向かって

歩いたそうです。その当時の沖縄は建物も少なく道路も山道で、思っていた以上に時間がかかったようです。私たちの待つ勝連に向かっていたのですが、北谷が米軍の攻撃にあったということで、本島南部の島尻方面へ行くようにと言われ、戻らされてしまったのです。母は祖母と四人の子どもを連れて、激戦地の南部の摩文仁をさまようことになってしまいました。

米軍の襲撃にあって、次兄と妹たちは亡くなりました。母は子どもたちを失って、戦場を逃げ惑っていました。それでも生き延びようと、母は祖母をおぶって本島北部の国頭村まで逃げたのですが、そこで祖母は栄養失調になって亡くなったそうです。母は守りたかった命の全てを失ってしまいました。

戦争が終わって一年近くたってから、母は勝連に戻ってきました。私は「妹はどうしたの?」と聞きました。母は顔面蒼白で言葉も出ません。母の体には爆弾の破片が残ったままでした。みんなが亡くなったのだと察しました。つらいことを聞いて母を余計に悲しませてはいけないと、長くその話はしませんでした。

三女の恵子は三歳でした。私をすごく慕っていました。母と島尻に逃げて、そこで命を落としました。母は瀕死の状態の子を助けたいと、おぶって逃げていたそうです。妹は亡

くなる時に、「光順にぃにぃ、光順にぃにぃ」と私の名前を呼びながら死んだということ

を後で母から告げられました。それを聞いた時は、とても悲しい気持ちになりました。

沖縄とアメリカの懸け橋に

勝連の疎開先の家には、ハワイ帰りのおじさんとおばさんが同居していました。ハワイ

で白人専用のタクシードライバーをしていたおじさんと、カメハメハ大王のメイドだった

おばさんです。料理も言葉も、全てハワイ仕込みでした。二人はハワイですごく儲かって、

那覇の泊に来て金物店を開業しました。それが戦争で追われて、勝連の私たちの実家に逃

れていたのです。二人は米軍の通訳をしていました。

戦後の沖縄は日本から切り離され、通貨も通用しない米軍の統治下にありましたから、

英語ができる通訳は大変に優遇されていました。米兵たちはお金ではなく、トラックの軍

車両に缶詰やお菓子をどっさりと持ってきてくれました。私たちは家の地下の部屋を貯蔵

所にして、食料などの物資を保管し、親戚に配っていました。二人が話す英語に米兵たち

が笑ったり、喜んだりしています。学校も始まっていなかったので、二人は私に英語とか

け算の九九を教えてくれました。米軍の将校が来たら、私もその中にちょこんと座らされ

て、一緒の時間を過ごしました。

勝連にいた時、十台から二十台ものトラックが列をなして通るのを見ました。南部の戦死者の遺体を、勝連のホワイトビーチから船で海に流していると通訳のおじさんに告げられました。私はその風景をじっと見ていましたが、信じられない気持ちでした。

戦争が終わった時に、海外生活の経験があった人と共同生活をすることになったことで、英語が耳にどんどん飛び込んでくる環境になっていました。高校に行った時には、校長の通訳ができるまで習得していました。その後も私は国際大学（現・沖縄国際大学）の一期生として学びました。いつしかウチナー（沖縄）とアメリカをつなげていく夢を描くようになっていました。私は普天間飛行場の司令官の通訳として働いた経験もあります。琉米親善に励んだこともありました。宜野湾市長の通訳の経験もしました。戦後も米軍と住民の両方に関わる人生を歩んできました。

ただ、戦争が終わっても、どの局面でも、排尿と便秘が私を襲いました。十・十空襲以来ずっと失禁と頻尿に苦しめられてきました。この苦しみは戦後七十四年の間、ずっと続いています。絶えず心が休まらないことばかりでしたが、今でも沖縄の県民が犠牲になることに味方したくないです。それは私の生涯を貫く決意となっています。

● 取材を終えて

南風原 宏明 さん

今回、光順さんの戦争体験を聞いて、沖縄戦の恐ろしさをあらためて知ることができました。

まず、「十・十空襲」では、軍・民の区別なく無差別に爆撃され、たくさんの人々が亡くなったという事実が強く印象に残りました。光順さんは、朝早くにご飯を食べようとしていたところに「空襲警報発令」と叫ぶ声を聞き、怖くて、はだしで箸（はし）を持ったまま逃げ出したそうです。その後近くの墓に入りましたが、そこでは身動きが取れず、八時間もトイレを我慢したと聞き、当時十歳の光順さんにとっては、とてもつらかっただろうなと思いました。

この空襲を境に、ぐっすり眠れなくなったり、排泄（はいせつ）障害が始まり、それが今でも続いているそうです。戦争の後遺症に苦しめられている人が今でも多くいると知り、とても驚きました。

戦後は、英語を勉強し、十年ほど米軍基地の中で通訳などもされたそうです。日本と世界を平和にしようと活動をしていることに感動しました。

これからは、自分たちが世の中の中心になっていきます。平和な世界を築いていくために身近な人を大切にし、次の世代に戦争はあってはならないということを伝えていきます。

大好きだった兄を
奪った戦争
——忘れることはできない

▷証言者 宮城 フジ子 さん
沖縄市在住／92歳

▶取材者 舟浮 聖 さん
高校1年生

舟浮 恋 さん
中学1年生

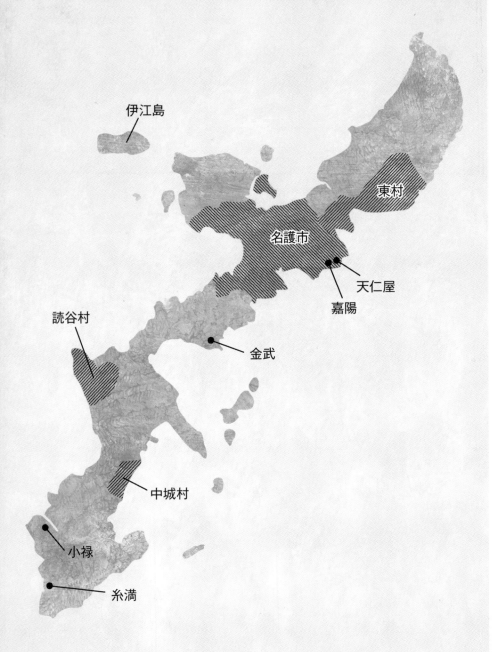

伊江島

東村

名護市

天仁屋

嘉陽

読谷村

金武

中城村

小禄

糸満

見張りと黒砂糖、竹やり訓練

一九二八（昭和三）年、久志村嘉陽（現・名護市嘉陽）で生まれました。私の家族は七人で、両親と兄が三人、私と妹です。

私は勉強が好きで、学校は一日も欠かさずに通いました。走るのも得意で、リレーでは第一走者を任されるほどでした。中学校ではバレーボールの選手でした。十三歳の時には名護の運動場で大きな大会があり、伊江島の中学校と対戦して、惜しくも二対一で負けたことも覚えています。

家の前は海でしたので、学校から帰ってくると、暇な時間は海で泳いで遊びました。そうして毎日を暮らしていました。

村では、戦争に備えて「見張り」がありました。大きな木に登って三人で交代しながら、飛行機が見えたら「戦争、敵機来襲！」と木の上から大声で村中に聞こえるように呼びかけました。「敵機来襲」という声が聞こえない日は、浜の畑に芋掘りに行きました。

当時好きなものは「黒砂糖」でした。家のそばには砂糖屋があって、さとうきびが並べ

てあり、機械で汁を搾って黒砂糖を作るのです。それを缶に入れて、子どもの手が届かないように、天井に上げてありました。本当はいけないことですが、私たちは入り口に見張りを立て、家の人に見つからないように天井に上り黒砂糖をくすねて食べていました。

学校の授業では竹やり訓練がありました。山からまっすぐに伸びた木を切ってきて、先を尖らせてやりを作ります。敵が来たら「敵機来襲」と言ってやりで突くんです。「エイ」「ヤー」と毎日一時間は訓練です。まっすぐな木で竹やりを作ろうと山に入った兄が、ハブに噛まれたこともありました。

戦争準備作業の合間に

　戦争の準備も手伝いました。日本軍からの命令です。父と一緒に伊江島に飛行場を造りに行きました。日本のハチマキをして、トラックに乗せられ港へ行き、そこから船で伊江島に連れていかれました。伊江島に着いたら、歩いて飛行場まで行きました。そこでは丸太で「よいしょ、よいしょ」と地面を打ち付ける作業が待っていました。二人一組で飛行場の滑走路を固める作業です。それが戦争の準備だったわけです。でも、私たちにはそれが戦争の準備とは知らされないでいました。そこでは、日本の兵隊はおいしい芋を食べて、

沖縄の人は虫のついた芋を食べさせられていました。

私は伊江島に文通している友達がいました。スミコさんという人で、バレーボールの試合で知り合いました。彼女も私も前衛センターのポジションで気持ちが通じ合い、すぐに仲良くなりました。友達になってからは嘉陽と伊江島とで文通を始めたのです。背が高い人でした。手紙にはバレーボールのことを書きました。「いつまでも友達でいようね」と約束していました。

私が伊江島へ作業に行った時も二人で会いました。「戦争は怖いね」「戦争が来ないようにするには、どうすればいいかな」などと話をしました。私は友達が好きだったから、一緒にいたいという気持ちがありました。墓のところで、持ってきた芋を食べました。虫の入った芋でしたが、二人でほじって食べたことはいい思い出です。友達と過ごす時間は、宝の時間でした。

スミコさんは戦争が始まったころ、私を訪ねて嘉陽に来たことがありました。私は芋や米などの食料を持たせました。

飛行場建設の作業が終わり自分の村へ帰るころには、日本軍があちこちに配備されているので余分なトラックなどはなく、自分たちで家まで歩いて帰りました。

召集された兄に会うために

「十・十空襲」では、山から低空飛行で来た戦闘機からの爆撃がありました。村の中心にある売店など五、六軒の家が焼けました。牛も豚も死にました。死んだ家畜は分けて食べました。中城から疎開していた女性二人が、その時に亡くなってしまいました。遺体からはすごい臭いがしました。敵は隣村の天仁屋に行ったと言われ、その隙に亡くなった人たちを埋めました。

空襲で私たちは山の中に避難しました。長兄にはその時に召集令状が来ました。山の中で千人針を作りましたが、完成する前に兄は二十歳で出征していきました（第二十四師団・通称「山部隊」に召集）。

私は大好きな兄が兵隊に取られ、心配でした。兄は読谷の部隊にいると聞き、読谷出身のおじさんの道案内で久志村嘉陽から読谷の陣地まで山を越えて、歩いて兄に会いに行きました。私は運動が得意で、足が丈夫ですから、全く苦ではありません。一人で歩いても、怖いものは何もありませんでした。兄が壕から出てくると、「近いうちにアメリカが来なければ、ソ連との戦いに備えて北海道に行く」と言うのです。私は「沖縄も戦争している

102

のに、北海道に行かないで」と泣きました。「これはしょうがないよ。軍が決めたことだから」と、兄は私をなだめました。私は読谷に二度、兄を訪ねました。

兄の部隊は読谷から島尻地区に移動していきました。私は歩いて島尻の兄のところにも会いに行きました。金武、那覇と南下しました。那覇では小禄にある同郷のおばさんの家に泊めてもらい、糸満まで三日がかりで行きました。

私が一人で会いに行ったのは、兄が元気なのか確かめるためです。私が糸満の陣地に訪ねていった時、面会で名前を伝えると「安谷屋」という沖縄の苗字に馴染みのない日本兵にはなかなか通じません。私は「違う、あだにや、安谷屋です」と言いました。ここまで来ているので、何としても兄に会いたいと懸命でした。兄は壕から出てきました。大切に持ってきた黒糖を兄に渡しました。それが兄との最後になりました。

兄の消息は長年わからなかった

大好きな兄がいつ亡くなったのか、わかりません。ずっと消息不明でした。兄の所属する中隊から生き残ったのは、わずか二人だということです。その方々が遺骨を集めて墓を作って弔ってく逃げずに壕に残り、そのまま亡くなったということでした。糸満で兄は

れていたのです。「安谷屋中郎　中三」——兄の名前の下に父の名が書かれ、その息子とわかるようにしてくれていました。見つけるのに長い時間がかかりました。近所の人づてに遺骨の場所を探し、一九八八（昭和六十三）年にやっと見つけました。戦争が終わって四十数年がたっていました。兄の消息は不明と思っていましたが、その時初めて戦死したということを実感しました。

　嘉陽では山の避難生活が続きました。私たち家族は、父も一緒でした。父はまだ若かったのですが、背が小さくて兵隊に合格しなかったそうです。一升瓶に玄米を入れて、竹でつついて精米する方法も、疎開中の山の中で父に教えてもらいました。

　アメリカの靴は音が高く「パッカ、パッカ」と隣の東村の方向から聞こえてきます。足音が近づいてきたら、山の深くに隠れました。雨の日に平石の陰に隠れていたら、石が壊れて埋まったこともありました。その時は帽子をかぶっていたので、息ができ助かりました。同級生のいとこと銀杏の木のそばに隠れたこともあります。隠れたつもりが、姿は丸見えで、「頭は隠して、お尻は見えてるさ」と二人で笑い合ったこともありました。

　戦争が終わる時は、おばあさんが竹に白いタオルをくくりつけ、みんなで山から下りて

戦争ほど怖いものはない

いきました。

戦争が終わった時は十八歳でした。私は長く編んだ髪を切りました。アメリカ兵に見つかったら、女の子はひどい目にあうと言われていたからです。だから怖くて、家に戻ってからも、タンスの中や仏壇の下にずっと隠れていました。

ある日、「大変だぞ、お前は兵隊の洗濯係になっている」と父に告げられました。米兵の軍服には虫がたくさんついていて洗うのは大変だから、洗濯係が必要だというのです。米兵たちが洗濯物を袋にかついでやってきました。私はとても嫌だったので、言うことを聞かずにいました。そうすると今度は、タバコとかお菓子とかいっぱい持ってきたんです。

米兵は、大きなたわしと石石鹸（固形石鹸）を持ってきました。「ユー、ワシワシ、オッケー?」と言って洗濯する仕草をやるわけです。そして「この石鹸は食べるものじゃないよ、ワシワシだよ」とやりとりしたことを今でも思い出します。こっちは木のやりで、米軍は機械や拳銃です。たくさん戦争というのは怖いものでした。

んの人が亡くなりました。戦争のことをいつでも思い出します。戦争がチャンバラか何かだと思っているのは、大きな間違いです。命に関わることをわからないとだめです。戦争ほど怖いものはない。戦争ほど怖いものはないのです。

● 取材を終えて

舟浮 聖 さん

今

回、フジ子さんが涙ながらに昔の記憶を思い出しながら語る姿を見て、本当に怖かったんだという思いがひしひしと伝わってきました。

もし、私がフジ子さんの立場に置かれたとしたら、身動きが取れなかったのではな

いかと思います。

このような戦争は、もう二度と起こしてはいけない。戦争以上に怖く恐ろしいことはないということを、あらためて知ることができて良かったです。

最近、県外に行く機会があり、フジ子さんと同世代の方にお会いする機会がありました。その際、「沖縄は戦争で大変だったのよ

ね」との言葉を聞いて驚きました。その方々は、沖縄戦があった時は小学校に通っており、地上戦は経験していないとのことでした。

戦争体験者が年々少なくなっていく中で、県外に住む私たちと同世代の中高生は、こうした話を聞く機会は、ほとんどないのではないかと思いました。沖縄で生まれ育ったからこそ、私たちには次の世代に伝えていく使命があるのだと感じました。

平和な未来を築いていくためにも、アメリカと日本、またその他の国の方々と差別なく平等に接していくことが大切だと思います。

また、日本だけでなく世界中の人にこのような戦争はもう二度と起こしてはいけな

い、戦争以上に怖く恐ろしいことはないということを、知ってほしいと思いました。

舟浮 恋 さん

今 回、宮城フジ子さんのお話を聞いて、私はすごいと思いました。フジ子さんは今の私と同年代で戦争を体験しています。フジ子さんは今の私と同年代で戦争を体験しています。妹の病気の時や兵隊になったお兄さんに会いに行く時も、遠くまで歩いていったと聞き、そこまでできるのは、今の若い人ではとても考えられないと思いました。フジ子さんは、心も体も強いと感じました。

フジ子さんは、戦争のお話を私たちに話してくれている時に、何回も何回も「戦争ほど怖いものはない」と言っていました。私も

学校で年に一度、戦争のことについて授業で学びます。戦争体験者の方のお話を聞く機会もありましたが、実際に体験者の暮らしや、どこに逃げてどうやって隠れていたのか等、こんなに詳しく聞くのは初めてでした。当時の情景やフジ子さんのその時の思いが聞けたので、イメージができて身近に感じることができました。

あらためて、本当に戦争ほど怖いものは

ないと強く思いました。今回、戦争を実際に体験したフジ子さんの話を聞けたことは、とてもいいことだったと思います。

また、戦争は怖いものなんだということを、伝えていける人になりたいです。平和である毎日が当たり前なのではなく、日々感謝をしながら、今できることを楽しんで大切に過ごしたいと思います。

本当は記憶から
消したい、
19歳のあの日々を

▷証言者 **与那嶺 ツル** さん
国頭郡今帰仁村在住／94歳

▶取材者 **與那覇 美月** さん
中学2年生

伊江島

仲原馬場

謝花

平敷

渡久地

与那嶺さんたちが避難した山地

今帰仁村

本部町

最後の徴兵検査を受けた学年だった

　私は沖縄本島北部の今帰仁村、平敷で生まれました。家は篤農家と呼ばれ、裕福でお手伝いさんもいました。私はひとりっ子で、両親との三人暮らし。小学校に入学すると、父は算数を教えてくれました。私はひとりっ子で、両親との三人暮らし。小学校に入学すると、父は算数を教えてくれました。墨をすって筆で毎晩のように教えてくれたおかげで、苦手な数字も書けるようになりました。母が再婚でしたので、実の娘でもない私を夢中になって育ててくれた父へ、感謝の気持ちでいっぱいです。

　今帰仁尋常高等小学校は、現在の仲原馬場のところにありました。本島北部の村ですが、生徒は四十人くらいいたと思います。中学にも三十人ほどが進学しました。

　私たちの同級生が一番損していると思ったりします。徴兵検査があったのは私たちの学年までです。私は女だから兵隊には行かなかったけれど、男子生徒は戦争に行かされて、多くの同級生が亡くなりました。

　中学卒業後は、大分の製糸工場に三年契約で働きに行きました。実家が養蚕をやっていましたので、母の後押しもありました。地元の友達も四、五人一緒でした。三年契約大分で生活して二年がたったころ、父から「帰ってこい」と手紙が来ました。三年契約

ですので、帰れるはずがありません。それでも父は、「娘は結婚させます」と嘘の手紙を会社に送り、私は半ば無理やり帰郷させられました。友達と離れ、一人で故郷・今帰仁村へ帰ってきたのです。十八歳でした。

空襲から逃げ続けた日々

一九四四（昭和十九）年には、「十・十空襲」がありました。私の記憶ではこれが沖縄戦の始まりと思います。

そのころ父は徴用されて、伊江島の飛行場の整備に行っていました。召集令状みたいなのが来るんです。それが来ると、忙しくても行かないといけません。十月になって、沖縄も少し肌寒くなってきたころでした。「寒くなっているから、着るものと毛布を持ってきてくれ」と父から連絡がありました。そしてご飯がおいしくないので、油味噌を作ってほしいという伝言でした。

伊江島の父のところへ私が持っていくことになりました。出発前夜に母が油味噌をこさえていると、伊江島に行くという噂を聞きつけて集落のおばさんたち二人がやってきました。その方たちも伊江島に家族がいると言うので、私と一緒に会いに出かけることになりた。

112

ました。

その日は朝九時の船に間に合わせるために、早くに起きて本部町の渡久地の港を目指しました。十キロほど歩いて、ちょうど本部町の謝花集落の坂道にさしかかった時のことです。飛行機が飛んできました。日本軍の飛行機だと思って喜んで万歳をしていると、「あれは友軍ではないぞ。アメリカーの飛行機だ!」「早く木の陰に隠れなさい」と自転車に乗った警防団員が村中に叫んでいました。びっくりして慌てて隠れました。この様子では伊江島行きの船に乗ることはできないかもしれないと不安に思っていると、渡久地の港のほうからボンボン、ボンボン、パラパラパラと砲弾の音が聞こえてきたのです。港は空襲でやられている、これは諦めるしかないと、私たち三人はもと来た道を引き返すことにしました。

帰り道でも空襲が続いています。飛行機が来たら木に隠れ、飛行機が遠ざかったら這い出してきて歩きました。私は学生時代にバレーボールなど運動の選手でもあったので、体力には自信がありました。ただ、自分だけならさっと逃げられますが、五十代のおばさん二人が一緒なので、急ぐこともできません。

家までもう少しのところまで来た時、飛行機が来ました。慌てて隠れようとしましたが、

田んぼの真ん中で、どこにも隠れるところがありません。引き返して松の木に隠れました。飛行機が遠ざかると川べりの土手を歩きました。するとまた飛行機がやってきました。土手には数本の桑の木がありましたが、葉がないので隠れることができません。それでも私はおばさん二人をなんとかその桑の木に隠して、自分は土手にへばりつきながら、周辺の雑草をちぎって頭や背中にのせ、少しでも目立たないようにと偽装しました。とにかく飛行機から見つからないようにと必死でした。ところが、必死の思いで隠したおばさんたちは、「怖い、怖い」と言って私のところに飛び出してきたのです。私は慌てて、おばさんたちに葉っぱをかけて隠し続けました。その繰り返しで、家に着いたのは午後五時になっていました。丸一日、逃げ続けていたのです。

集落内では空襲はなかったようで、警防団が警戒に回っていました。家に母はいませんでした。家の中はぐちゃぐちゃで、タンスから出したものは、そのままほったらかされているような状態でした。母も慌てて逃げたのでしょう。私は湯のみをカバンに入れ、すぐに防空壕に行きました。

母は出かけたままの私を心配して、お昼も食べずに防空壕の入り口に座っていたそうです。戻ってきた私を見つけて、抱きついてきました。逃げ続けた長い一日でした。

戦争の始まり

空襲の後、しばらくして伊江島から父が帰ってきました。それからしばらくは平穏な日々が続いたので、戦争が来るとは思っていませんでした。

ところがある日、また空襲が始まったのです（注：一九四五〈昭和二十〉年四月一日、米軍が沖縄本島中部西海岸に上陸。同月十日には、今帰仁村に進攻した）。今度は、家にいては危ないと山へ隠れました。空襲はどんどん激しさを増していきました。

朝から艦砲射撃がボンボン打ち込まれ、午後三時ごろは山へ向けてひっきりなしの攻撃でした。するとその後、急に静かになりました。戦争ではないくらいに静かなんです。おしっこをしに行ったおばさんが、「友軍が来た」と母へ告げました。戦争ではなく、友軍が来れば安心だと思った母は外に出ていったそうです。ところが来たのは友軍ではなく、アメリカ兵でした。

艦砲射撃の後、米軍がいよいよ上陸したのでしょう。住民は山に逃げていたので、米軍は悠々と村に入ってこられただろうと言われていました。

私たち家族の防空壕は、一般的な縦穴に追加して横穴が掘られていました。それは父の指示でした。中の配置にも父の指示がありました。横穴の入り口正面にはものを置き、人

は横穴の中に隠れるようにと。さらに防空壕の入り口は木の枝を植えて隠されています。壕の中には母とおばあさんと叔母たち、私といとこの静子、憲の女子ども七人が入っていました。いとこの憲は四歳で、私がずっとおぶっていました。静子は小学三年生でした。

父は警戒して壕の前の土手で見張りをしていました。

とうとう私たちの防空壕の前にも米軍がやってきました。米軍は手榴弾を三発、防空壕へ投げ入れました。それから手早く乾いた木の枝に火をつけて燃やしていきます。中にいる私たちは、煙を吸わないように口を押さえてじっとしていました。八十歳のおばあさんは寝ていたので、状況がわからず「ヌーガーヌーガー（どうしたどうした）」と言って騒ぎ立てました。どうしようもないので、口を押さえました。

一父は手榴弾を投げ込まれるのを表で見ていたんで、どうして自分一人が生き残ってしまったのか」と泣いていたそうです。ところが防空壕にいる私たちは横穴に隠れていたので、爆弾の直撃を免れていました。中でじっとしていたのですが、夕方になり米兵は立ち去ったのではないかと思い、外に出ることにしました。最初に私が様子を見に出ていきました。その後ぞろぞろと全員が壕から出てきました。父はそれを見て、「したいひゃー（でかした）」と喜んだといいます。

山での避難生活

父は区長をしていました。もしもの時に備えて、大切な村の書類をブリキの箱に入れ、石垣の中に隠していました。戦争が終わった後に、書類が残っているとみんな喜んでいました。これは鮮明に覚えています。

山での避難生活が続きます。昼間は山に避難していますが、夕方からは飛行機が飛ばないので、みんな山を下り、食べ物の準備や洗濯などのために村に戻っていました。用をすませると夜遅くか朝早くに山へ登ります。私は運動で鍛えた体で、食料を取りに家と山を二往復していました。

ある日、村から山の途中まで戻ってきた時に、アメリカの飛行機が飛んできました。山に入るのを見られたら、機関銃を打ち込まれて家族が危険な目にあってしまう。私はとっさに近くにあったソテツの下に隠れました。トゲのあるソテツの幹を抱いていると、私をめがけて機関銃が撃ち込まれました。弾が葉っぱに当たります。右にパラパラと聞こえたら左に逃げ、左に音がしたら反対側にとぐるぐるとソテツの周りを逃げ回りました。母は山の上から標的になる私の様子を見て泣いたそうです。父も、まばたきもせずにずっと見

ていたそうです。ぐるぐると回って逃げ惑っているうちに、飛行機は他所（よそ）へ飛んでいきま

した。ほっとしてソテツから飛び出してきた時には、父は「ツルが出た！」と叫び、母と

喜び合ったそうです。私は平然とかごを持って、ゆっくりゆっくりと山を登っていきまし

た。これが私の一番怖かった経験です。

そこからは戦闘はそう長くはなかったです。米兵がメガホンで、片言交じりの日本語で

「戦争終わりました。もう大丈夫です。家に戻ってください」と放送していました。最初

は出たら殺されると思って、素直に家に戻りませんでした。女の子は米兵に見られたらみ

んな乱暴されると言われていました。草わらびが高く生えている場所に、一人入れるくら

いの隠れ場所を父が作ってくれて、私は一人で隠れていました。

山に米兵がやってきた時も、私は草わらびの隙間（すきま）から父たちの様子を見ていました。米

兵に捕まった時、父は殺されると思っているようでした。米兵がポケットから日の丸を出

して地面に置き、「踏みなさい」と言っているように見えました。父が日の丸を踏むと、

米兵は笑って肩を叩（たた）いていました。父はすごく傷ついて、戦後もこのことを悔（く）いていまし

た。そのたびに、「あの時踏まなかったら、生きていなかったでしょう」と母が慰（なぐさ）めてい

ました。夕方になって米兵たちがいなくなってから、明日は家に帰ろうと山を下りたので

す。

米兵から隠れて過ごした日々

　山を下りた後も、私は米兵に見つからないようにと、離れの物置小屋の天井に隠されていました。食事も天井に鍋を引っ張り上げて食べていました。夕方になったら隠れている天井から下りていくという生活です。一カ月ほどしたら、離れの天井ではさびしいだろうと母屋の天井に移動されました。

　そのころ、私の家には疎開していた人たちが一緒に暮らしていました。日ごろは仕事もないので、山であったことの思い出話などおしゃべりをして過ごしていました。私一人だけが隠れ部屋で生活しているのを、父は不憫に思ったのでしょう。今度は天井から仏壇の下の戸袋に移動させられ、壁に小さな穴を開けて、みんなの様子を見たり聞いたりできるようにしてくれました。そこで三カ月ほど過ごしました。私がまだ隠れていることを聞きつけた友達が、「もう出ても大丈夫だよ」と教えに来てくれて、やっと隠れ部屋を出るようになりました。

　それでも外へ出る時は、若い女性であることがばれないように、鍋の底の油やすすでク

リームを作って、真っ黒な顔で歩きました。ある日、母の手伝いで芋洗いをしていました。すると米兵が二人来たんです。私は初めて間近で見る米兵にびっくりしていました。彼らは私に気がつくと、近寄ってきました。そして黒い顔を見て、大きな声で笑いました。米兵たちに気づいてないふりをして、背中を向けて芋をかごの中に投げ込んでいました。洗面器に水を入れて持ってきて、私の前に置き、顔を洗う仕草（しぐさ）をします。私は観念してさっと顔を洗いました。米兵たちは笑顔になるとそのまま立ち去っていきました。恐怖で怯え（おび）る毎日でしたが、中にはいい人もいるんだと思いました。そしてこの時から、私は隠れずに生活することになりました。

戦争体験を話すことを、最初はどうしようかと迷いました。でも話さなかったら、後悔すると思い、話すようになりました。こんな怖かったこと、若い人たちに言いたくないんです。本当は記憶から消したいです。

戦争の苦しみは、経験しないとわからないことだと思います。でも、戦争のことを考える時、おばあ（＝自分のこと）を思い出してほしいです。今日のおばあの話を思い出してください。私は九十四歳。十九歳にあった戦争のことを、この長い年月、忘れたことはないのです。

● 取材を終えて

與那覇 美月 さん

㊙がツルさんの戦争体験を聞いて、一番心に残っている話は、防空壕(ごう)に隠れている時、アメリカ軍に手榴弾(しゅりゅうだん)を投げ込まれた話です。

防空壕はツルさんのお父さんが造ったもので、まっすぐに続く穴だけではなく、曲がり角も作られていたそうです。ツルさんは、曲がり角のところで口を手で押さえながら隠れていたと言っていました。想像しただけでとても怖くて、それを体験したツルさんたちはもっと怖かっただろうなと思いました。

ほかにもいろいろな体験を聞きましたが、ツルさんが若いからとみんなをリードして、守る役割をしていたと知り、すごいなと思いました。ツルさん自身、精神もボロボロになっていたはずです。それでも、生きるためにみんなを引っ張って逃げたのは、本当にすごくて、私にはできないことだなと感じました。

私の考えているリーダーシップのある人とは、みんなに平等に接することのできる人、いろいろな考えを持っている人の意見をまとめる力のある人ではないかと思います。また、戦争という非常事態の中で、命を守るために、リーダーシップを取ることのできたツルさんの勇気に感動しました。戦争は残酷(ざんこく)です。二度と戦争は起こしてはいけないと思いました。私は戦争を体験したことがないので、本当の意味で戦争の怖さ

や苦しみはわからないかもしれません。け
れども、私が聞いた戦争体験を、次の世代に
も語り続けていくことはできますし、そう
していきたいと思います。

ツルさんの戦争体験を本人から聞くこと
ができた貴重な経験を忘れずに、どのよう
に伝えていくことができるかを考えていき
たいです。また、私の祖母からも疎開先で経

験した戦争体験を直接聞くことができるの
で、ツルさんの話と比較してみたいです。

祖母が戦争中に感じていたことやこれか
らの世の中に期待していることなどを大切
にして、平和のために行動できることを見
つけていきたいと思います。私一人の小さ
な行動かもしれないけれど、続けていくこ
とが大切だと思います。

むすびにかえて

　創価学会沖縄青年部は、これまで取り組んできた平和運動とともに、自分たちからさらに後の世代へと、「未来へつなげる平和運動」について、模索しながら、挑戦してきました。その一つが、このたび、本書として結実した沖縄未来部による沖縄戦体験の聞き取り運動です。

　二〇一六年に発刊された『未来へつなぐ平和のウムイ（思い）』は、青年部が中心となって聞き取りを行いましたが、今回中心となったのは、沖縄の新しい時代を担っていく中・高等部（中高生）のメンバー。戦後七十五年がたち、戦争体験を語る人がいなくなってしまう時が近づく中、今回、沖縄戦の体験者にお会いし、直接の聞き取りができた意義は非常に大きいと感じています。本書を通して、将来を担う若い世代の方々の胸に、平和を希求する「沖縄のククル（心）」が受け継がれていくことを強く願っています。

　二〇一八年、沖縄青年部は「世界青年平和文化祭」を、沖縄コンベンションセンター

（宜野湾市）で開催し、青年世代を中心に一万五千人が集い合うことができました。沖縄に

は、「命どぅ宝（命こそ宝）」「ユイマール（助け合い）」「チムグクル（相手を思いやる心）」「イチャリバチョーデー（行き

逢えば皆、兄弟）」など、先人たちが残した「沖縄のククル」を象

徴する言葉があります。文化祭では、こうした言葉に込められた精神性をもとに、沖縄

に生きる私たち青年が、人と人、心と心を結ぶ「結の心」で、あらゆる差異を超えて手を

携えていくことを誓い合いました。

今回の沖縄戦体験の聞き取り運動の中心を担ってくれたのは、この平和文化祭に出演、

参加した未来部のメンバーです。さらに、これからの「戦争を知らない世代」が、沖縄戦

を語り伝えていけるよう、聞き取りをした沖縄戦の証言をもとに、紙芝居の制作も進めて

います。

今、私たちは、「戦争の記憶」を風化させることなく、沖縄の「平和の心」を未来へつ

なげていけるかどうかの分岐点にいます。今こそ、若い世代へ、平和の重要性を伝え、と

もに成長していくための運動を継続的に展開していこうと決意しています。

池田ＳＧＩ（創価学会インタナショナル）会長は、今から六十年前、一九六〇（昭和三十五）

年七月に沖縄を初めて訪れ、南部戦跡を視察しました。戦禍の傷跡を目の当たりにし、「最も苦しんだ沖縄こそ、最も幸福になり、最も平和になる権利がある」との思いで、沖縄の地で小説『人間革命』の執筆を開始しました。

『人間革命』の主題は、「一人の人間における偉大な人間革命は、やがて一国の宿命の転換をも成し遂げ、さらに全人類の宿命の転換をも可能にする」との哲理です。池田会長の「不戦の誓い」のバトンを受け継ぐ私たち青年が、この哲理を根本に、誠実な対話を通して、身近なところから、行動を積み重ねていくこと。そして、平和建設の主体者となる後継の人材を輩出していくことこそ、世界平和への確かな一歩であることを確信し、さらなる平和のスクラムを日本中、世界中に広げていきます。

最後に、本書の出版にあたりご尽力いただいた第三文明社をはじめ、ご協力いただいた体験者の皆さま、沖縄未来部、沖縄青年平和委員会、女性平和文化会議の皆さまに心から感謝申し上げます。

二〇二〇年六月

創価学会沖縄青年部長　前島　常仁

Copyright © The Soka Gakkai 2020

Published in Japan in 2020
by Daisanbunmei-sha, Inc.
1-23-5 Shinjuku Shinjuku-ku, Tokyo Japan
https://www.daisanbunmei.co.jp/

私がつなぐ沖縄のククル

2020年 9月 7日　　初版第 1 刷発行

編　者　創価学会沖縄未来部
発行者　大島光明
発行所　株式会社 第三文明社
　　　　東京都新宿区新宿1-23-5
　　　　郵便番号　160-0022
　　　　電話番号　03(5269)7144(営業代表)
　　　　　　　　　03(5269)7145(注文専用)
　　　　　　　　　03(5269)7154(編集代表)
　　　　振替口座　00150-3-117823
　　　　Ｕ Ｒ Ｌ　https://www.daisanbunmei.co.jp/
英語翻訳　日笠 誠
装幀・本文レイアウト　村上ゆみ子
編集協力　鳥越一枝／株式会社クリエイティブメッセンジャー
印刷・製本　中央精版印刷株式会社

Connecting to the Heart of Okinawa

Soka Gakkai Okinawa Future Division

DAISANBUNMEI-SHA

Preface

The Battle of Okinawa was so horrific that it is said to have "brought together in one place all the hell that could be found in the world." The beautiful sea was filled with warships, and the "typhoon of steel" caused by air raids and naval gunfire changed the nature of the lush island.

The Soka Gakkai's Okinawa Youth Division has been working to convey the experience of the war to the next generation with the pledge of "war must never happen again."

In June 1974, the Soka Gakkai Okinawa Youth Division interviewed those who had experienced the Battle of Okinawa and published the first book of war experiences, *Shattered Uruma Island*.

In February of the same year while visiting Okinawa, Daisaku Ikeda, President of the Soka Gakkai International, met with representatives of junior high and senior high school students. He told them, "Today, the memory of war is being forgotten by society. That is why I urge you, for the sake of the 21st century, to painstakingly remember the suffering of your fathers and mothers. We have a mission, a responsibility, and a duty to pass on."

"As time passes, the true impact of war is forgotten and buried in history. The truth will not be conveyed unless it is written down. Therefore, for the sake of peace, I would like you to leave behind a collection of testimonies about your experiences in order to convey the 'heart of Okinawa.' This is my sincere wish."

Accepting SGI President Ikeda's proposal, members of the junior and senior high school students took time out of their club activities and studies to talk with their parents and neighbors about their war experiences.

There must have been many sleepless nights after they listened to the tragic stories of those who had experienced the war. In assembling the stories into a book, they were reminded of the ugliness of war and they renewed their commitment to building peace. The interviews by those junior and senior high

school students were compiled into a collection of testimonies entitled *The Bloodstained Kariyushi Sea* in June 1976.

Last year (2019), to commemorate the 75th anniversary of the Battle of Okinawa, the Okinawa Future Division again worked with junior and senior high school students. Fifteen students interviewed eight survivors of the war, collecting their war experiences.

The survivors were between the ages of 9 and 19 at the time of the Battle of Okinawa. They experienced the war when they were the same age as the members of the junior and senior high school students who interviewed them.

They often said, "War is wrong." The words of those who experienced the war firsthand touched our hearts deeply. After the interviews, each student decided that they would strive to pass on the idea of peace to the next generation. This book includes the student interviewers' thoughts following each survivor's experience. In order to bring the invaluable testimonies in this book to the world, an English translation of the entire book has been created.

It would be our joy if this collection of testimonies is able to convey to the next generation the "heart of Okinawa" that "war must never happen again" and help to build solidarity for world peace.

June 2020

Keisuke Yamaguchi
Okinawa Future Division Chief

Yukino Kamiya
Okinawa Young Women's Future Division Chief

CONTENTS

Chronology of the Battle of Okinawa

1944

March 22	Japanese Imperial Headquarters established Thirty-second Army (Lieutenant General Masao Watanabe in command).
April 15	Thirty-second Army orders construction of airfields on Ie Island and Miyako Island in Okinawa.
July 7	Saipan falls.
August 10	Lieutenant General Mitsuru Ushijima replaces Watanabe as commander of Thirty-second Army.
August 22	Attacked by US submarine, student evacuation ship *Tsushimamaru* sinks near Akuseki Island; over 1482 killed, including about 784 students.
October 10	US task force conducts air raid on Nansei (Ryukyu) Islands; indiscriminate bombing of Naha burns 90 percent city. (Note: Naha is the seat of the Okinawa Prefectural Government located in the southwest of Okinawa Island)
December 9	Thirty-second Army starts building headquarters in caves under Shuri Castle. (Note: Shuri was capital of Ryukyu Kingdom (1429-1879))
December 14	Thirty-second Army forces Okinawa Prefectural Government to order all women and elderly residing in central or south Okinawa Island to evacuate north; all those capable of fighting are ordered to join battle under the Nansei Islands Home Guard.

1945

February 9	US Army launches Operation Iceberg.
February 10	Governor Akira Shimada directs 100,000 residents of central and south Okinawa Island to evacuate north.
March 23	US military strikes all of the Southwest Islands.

March 24	US fleet opens artillery fire on Okinawa Island.
March 26	US troops land on Zamami and two neighboring islands. Residents on Geruma and Zamami islands commit mass suicide.
March 27	US troops land on three more islands, including Tokashiki.
March 28	Mass suicide on Tokashiki Island.
End of March	Students in 21 Okinawa middle schools mobilized as "Student Corps of Blood and Iron for the Emperor" and sent to the front.
April 1	US troops land at Chatan and Yomitan villages on the west coast of Okinawa Island.
April 3	US Army divides Okinawa Island; deploys troops north and south.
April 19	US troops break defensive line between Ginowan and Urasoe.
May 5	Japanese army fails all-out attack; defeat of Japanese army becomes certain.
May 22	Thirty-second Army Headquarters abandons Shuri and withdraws to the south.
June 19	Thirty-second Army Commander Ushijima issues final order: "Fight bravely to the end and go to everlasting life for our cause." The end of organized fighting.
June 23	Commander Ushijima commits suicide.
June 25	Imperial Headquarters declares the end of Okinawa Operation.
August 15	Japan's unconditional surrender.
September 7	US Army and Japanese Survival Unit sign instrument of surrender.

Telling the Truth about the War is Difficult because War Is Too Cruel

Survivor: **Takeshi Itokazu** Residing in Naha City / 86 years old
Interviewer: Ibuki Nishizato   First Year in Senior High School

A strict father and a mother who likes movies

I was born in 1933 at Kami Izumi, Naha City (present day Kumoji). My parents were blessed with a child as they grew older and my whole family was so delighted to see me come into the world.

Whenever my parents would go to the Obon festival (commemoration of ancestors), New Year celebration, or visiting relatives or friends, they would always take me with them. My father, Shoei, had served in the Japanese Navy and thus he was very strict. I had a very strict upbringing by my father. If I came home crying after fighting at school, my father would get very angry. So, I would wait until my tears had dried before coming home. When I was scolded by my father he would usually strike me; it was just like being in the military. However, I liked writing Japanese characters and when I tried my best, practicing my writing in a notebook, my father would always compliment me. At such times he would lavish me with overwhelming praise.

My mother Etsuko really loved watching movies and we went a couple of times. Those times I really enjoyed riding on a rickshaw. In those days, movies at a theater reflected the Japanese militarism of the time and just before the movie they would show the military news on the screen. When they showed scenes of the Japanese military marching victoriously in the regions of Southeast Asia, the audience applauded joyfully. When I think about it now, this was how the Japanese military authorities propagated

military education on the people of the nation.

I first attended Koshin Normal Elementary School in Naha City and in the summer after 4th grade I transferred to Sobe National School, also in Naha City. In the neighborhood of Sobe there were still farming fields and inside the school grounds there were fields that grew Japanese white radishes, carrots and green vegetables. We students watered the plants, spread fertilizer and sometimes pulled weeds, gaining the experiencing of working in the fields. Even though I transferred from an elementary school in the city, I was able to quickly make new friends here.

Periodically the soldiers working in logistics would come to our school. They would chop down trees, make sheds and care for their horses. I gained the impression that soldiers think a great deal about their horses and value them highly.

We upper-class students were tasked with cutting leaves to cover the roof of the stable. I didn't have much experience in this type of work. Seeing me doing this job so slowly, my country-raised classmates taught me how to trim them more quickly.

At school it was prohibited to speak in the Okinawan local dialect and we were all forced to speak standard Japanese. If we carelessly spoke in Okinawan dialect without thinking, we would be punished by hanging a sign around our necks. This was considered a source of humiliation.

Living in a fierce military situation

In 1944 I was 11 years old and was in the 5th grade in elementary school. Around February, a student evacuation to mainland Japan was begun. Teachers were to supervise all students and parents were not allowed to go with their children. And so, many parents and children were separated. As the evacuation entered its final stage, mothers were allowed to evacuate with their children. My father wanted my mother and me to evacuate to Kagoshima Prefecture, but my mother was fiercely against it. My mother insisted that even if we were to encounter the most dangerous of

situations, our family should all stay together no matter what. Therefore, our family was one of those who remained on Okinawa.

October 10th of that same year happened to be a Sunday. It was a very clear day without a cloud in the sky. At around 10:00 a.m. I was playing with a group of friends, who had also remained in Okinawa, when we heard the deafening roar of airplanes. Two or three of us kids climbed up in a pine tree to get a better look. We were thinking it was a training flight but suddenly we saw white smoke from the machine guns in the formation of planes as they made a steep descent and started bombing. It was directed towards Naha harbor and Naha airfield. Next we saw the flames shooting out from an antiaircraft gun firing from Kanagusuku in Naha City. Then, the loud screech of a siren sounded and a loud voice announced, "Prepare for attack from the enemy!" We quickly climbed down from the tree and ran home at top speed.

As soon as we arrived home we all donned our air defense hoods as quickly as possible and jumped into an air raid shelter, a hole we had dug out in front of our house. As we had trained daily, we placed our thumbs in our ears and covered our eyes with the rest of our fingers. We didn't really know how much time had passed, but the air raid siren stopped in the evening and we nervously came out from the shelter like a bunch of moles. Everyone wore a scared look on their face.

Our house was twelve doors from the Nichumae marketplace and remained in perfect condition. That was a miracle. Buildings lining the streets of Naha were still burning. The situation was still dangerous so we decided to wait until after dark and then go to the old Mawashi Village in Shikina for evacuation. When we got there, it was crowded with refugees and there was no place for our family to rest in peace. We gave up and went back home.

Driven away from our residence as our family became separated

March 23, 1945 came and right after finishing breakfast I heard a loud

"bang, bang" noise like a drum far away. Soon, a soldier came and told us, "Enemy warships have started bombardment in Minatogawa, Shimajiri District. They will probably come to land. If we stay here it will be too dangerous so it would be better to evacuate to a bigger shelter." My father had a navy background and he also decided that if we stayed here it would be too dangerous so we decided to flee.

I poured water into a canteen and strapped a first aid kit across my shoulder in preparation for departure. Since we were trained daily in preparation for the war, I was able to do it quickly. The only thing I was thinking about was running away.

We decided to go to the shelter nearby our house in Jyogaku area. However, one week later Japanese soldiers directed us to move out from the shelter because it was built by the military. We civilians had no choice but to leave; at that time we could not object to the Japanese soldiers. Since my father was an organizing chief for a ward in the community, he had contacts with people in the town office and we decided to relocate to a shelter behind the old Mawashi Village office.

There were already twelve people, three households, evacuated there. My parents pleaded with these people and at last our entire family was allowed to go into the shelter. The people were very kind and even shared their cooked rice and gave us tea to drink. Since we were famished their kindness was greatly appreciated. Outside, battle unfolded across the area, but inside the shelter we were able to make our daily life in a friendly atmosphere.

The American enemy used light planes to scout for Japanese military positions, calling in the full attack from the U.S. warships. Most of the vegetation was blown away by the bombardment from the warship and the landscape became naked, covered in gray. I intently watched the situation in silence. I saw half of a hill in the distance vanish due to the full attack from warships and even though I was still a small child at the time, I realized how serious this was. I quietly listened to the adult's conversations but I could not imagine that the whole island was

surrounded by U.S. warships.

Needless to say, the bombardment by warship continued and soon rifle bullets were whistling as they flew by. Due to his experience in the navy, upon hearing the sound of bullets my father recognized that the U.S. military was drawing near and he warned everyone. Rather than become prisoners of war, we decided to flee to Shimajiri area.

Just before departure, my father's stomach was in pain and he told my mother and me that we should go with the others and he would follow later. My mother and I told him that we would wait until he felt better but my father said this would cause everyone trouble and he wouldn't listen to us. After a heated argument my mother told my father that we would go first but for him to please come soon. She followed the group of people from the shelter. As it would happen, these were the last words that I exchanged with my mother and it was my final parting with her. At first I couldn't decide whether I should go with my mother or stay with my father but I could not leave my father alone in his condition and I decided to stay with him. Thirty minutes later my father and I started to walk and followed after them. We thought we would be able to follow them sooner but we could not.

The Madan Bridge that connected Naha and the southern part of the island was the scene of a gathering of a large crowd of refugees. To escape to the southern part of the island you must cross the Kokuba River. The bridge had been damaged in two places by the Japanese military. My father grabbed my hand and going up and down the damaged bridge we finally reached the other side. I was hoping to see my mother there. Looking around there were many people who were shouting names searching for family members who had become separated. Since I was longing to see my mother I shouted, "Mother! Mother!" and also loudly shouted her full name, "Etsuko Itokazu!" However, we were scolded by a Japanese soldier saying, "Don't shout! Hurry and escape! Be quick and go!" and we were driven away by Japanese soldiers and had no choice but to give it up our search. Where did my mother go after leaving the shelter?

After that time, I never saw my mother again.

The truth of war is too cruel

Even though we were trying to escape there was no clear destination for us. In any case we were all heading towards the southern part of the island and wherever the group was heading, we simply followed them. Not just one or two people, but as a group we all tried to escape. Since there was no food to eat we would dig in the ground for potatoes and we would even eat leaves to keep up our strength. At night we went to draw water to drink and in the day, everywhere we looked there were many dead bodies.

I saw dead people along the roadside many times. When people die, gas is formed from their body tissues and they swell up to the size of a calf. Imagine if you mistakenly step on a dead body, their skin comes off and the smell of the body sticks to you and it doesn't come off.

I have seen a body half blown away from an explosion and a hand hanging down from a tree. Even though I saw these cruel scenes, the only thing that came to my mind was, we would be like this if it happened to us. After my experiences in war, even now when someone dies I don't feel any fear.

One day, a bomb dropped near us. There was a 20-year-old young lady who was evacuating together with us. Many fragments from the bomb hit her in the back and she was groaning in pain. She was moaning throughout the night but by the next morning she finally died. A compassionate group of people placed her body in the hole caused by the bomb and covered her with dirt. I was deeply moved by their behavior in the midst of the risk to our lives while trying to escape the war. I could only think about how to live through the fire and destruction of war. That was the only thing I could contemplate. At one point, I was hit by a bullet. I thought something had struck me but at the time I felt no pain. After a while I did start to feel pain. A bullet had entered through my buttock and exited from my inner thigh. My father took the tincture of iodine from the first aid kit I had brought

and applied it as a temporary measure.

Once, I had seen a living human infested with maggots. I couldn't believe this person was using a pair of chopsticks made from a bamboo branch to pick a maggot from his arm. Since I applied an ointment to my wounds they didn't fester and I was not infested with maggots. I did have pain in my leg and dragged my feet on the ground, but there were no lasting effect from my injury.

Once, we ran into a shelter searching for a place to stay. There was a Japanese soldier who pointed his rifle towards us and said if we didn't leave within five minutes he would kill us. Even though I was just a child at the time, I felt angry that the Japanese soldiers did not protect anyone.

There we were, right in the middle of the battle wondering whether we would be killed by an artillery shell or a soldier. I was losing hope and my will to live. I was watching with a strange calmness and thinking that this must be the reality of war.

Final parting with my father

By the middle of June the war had come to the Makabe and Arakaki area. Bombardment from the warships was becoming more fierce, covering the entire area. Even though we were inside a shelter, the tremendous sound of the explosions continually split our ears.

We came across a strong trench that was carved into rock and we pleaded for the occupants to allow the two of us to hide inside. Others who could not find better shelter placed boards against the top of a stone wall to hide under for survival. Nearby, elderly ladies leaned a sheet of galvanized steel from the top of a stone wall, covered it in dirt and hid beneath. When the bombardment eased, my father told me there was a person nearby with an injured arm and he took the first aid kit and ran out to treat the wound. Ten minutes later the fierce bombardment began again.

After the bombing stopped there was no indication that my father would return. Some of the people hiding in the same trench went outside

to check and when they came back they said they found my father but he was not responding. They suggested, "You should go see for yourself." Just then I had a bad feeling that something had happened to my father. I went out and saw my father leaning up against a rock wall. I repeatedly called out saying, "father, father," but he did not respond. Even as I shook his body there was no response. I found his body was cold and I realized that my father had passed away.

I went back to the shelter where everyone was hiding and cried loudly. Everyone probably knew that my father had already passed away. They said to me, "If you had died first, your father would no longer have a reason live." and, "As long as you are alive you can memorialize your father."

My heart was filled with feelings of sorrow and anxiety and I couldn't stop my tears. I had been separated from my mother, I never saw her again. I had clung to my father and survived through the battle up to this point. I was now alone and the people in the shelter tried their utmost to encourage me in any way possible.

Remarkably, the day after the passing of my father, the artillery and bombardment stopped. That morning began a very fine day and I was dazzled by the bright sunlight.

Even now I still remember vividly the night before my father died. During a break in the bombardment, while the U.S. soldiers were taking a short rest, my father felt that it was a good time for a talk so he took me outside. We sat down at on a small bank on the side of the trench and both of us looked up at the sky. We saw a starlit sky for the first time in ages.

My father spoke slowly. He said, "Takeshi, what I'm going to tell you now is very important so please listen carefully. If we lose this war and became prisoners, the Americans might kill an adult but I don't think they would kill a child. But still, if they decide to torture you in some way or another I will teach you a very simple way to die without any pain. Just like going to sleep." Upon hearing this I nodded. Then my father gave me a hug. Ever since the evacuation had started my father had never spoke such things to me. I still wonder why my father spoke to me like this just

before he happened to die.

Daily life after becoming a prisoner of war

After that, I stayed with a doctor who was from Hamamatsu. One day a
military tank passed by a hundred meters in the distance. The American
soldiers walking behind the tank rushed over to us as soon as they saw us.
As I watched, I stood up and tried to run away but the doctor grabbed my
pants and pulled me down as he said, "Don't move. Be still."

The soldier gave me emergency provisions. I tried to eat a biscuit but
the doctor said, "Just a minute," and stopped me. Then the American
soldier tasted a biscuit to show it was not poisoned. Relieved after seeing
this, we ate the biscuit together. At that time, I felt I had never tasted such
a delicious treat as this. On that day, I became a prisoner of war. As I was
about to ride in a transport after becoming a prisoner, I realized that I had
made it, I had lived through this war.

After becoming a prisoner, I was transferred to several different
locations by truck. I was completely alone. Even at the prisoner camp
when we were lined up by groups, I was alone. Then I heard someone call
out to me. It was Mr. Ishibashi, a friend of my father. He said, "Are you
alone? Where is your father?" I responded by saying, "My father passed
away. I was separated from my mother and don't know what happened to
her after that." Mr. Ishibashi said to me, "I see. In that case, come with us."

Mr. Ishibashi was my father's acquaintance when my father was the head
chief of the ward. I had visited his house together with my father. Before
the war, I performed a dance at Mr. Ishibashi's house and he remembered
me.

After that I lived together with the Ishibashi family. At first I didn't have
any feelings of joy or sorrow. I simply felt that he was not a stranger and so
I didn't feel uncomfortable.

Even after we left the prisoner camp and went back to Naha, Mr.
Ishibashi gave me a home and took good care of me. It was he who

ensured I received an education from the 5th grade in elementary school up through senior high school. He became my foster parent.

Mr. Ishibashi taught me many things, sparing me from feeling ashamed in life. I learned how to harvest potatoes and pull weeds. The Ishibashi family had fields in Naha and I kept busy raising goats, pulling weeds, chopping firewood, taking care of domestic animals, and collecting water in an oil drum for everyday use. It turned out that learning to pull weeds during my days at Sobe Elementary School was very useful after all.

Even though I became a war orphan, thanks to the Ishibashi family I didn't feel deprived at all as I was raised in a family with connections to my father. I feel that I was blessed with such a happy life. I have the deepest appreciation to Mr. Ishibashi who really took good care of me after the war. I exist today because of my parents. Even now, every day I express my sense of appreciation for my parents.

After the Interview **Ibuki Nishizato**

After hearing Mr. Itokazu's war experience I have tried to compare my own present circumstances with his battle to survive the war and find a peaceful existence. It is shocking to consider our daily life eating delicious foods every morning, lunch and dinner, spending our days learning at school, and enjoying our smartphones compared to what Mr. Itokazu endured during the war.

When listening to his talk, he mentioned the names of places like Nichumae and Mawashi and while thinking of these present day locations I imagined them during the frightening days of war.

It is frightening just to think about how the scene changed from the dark of night to the bright of day. In the safety of the night when the military was taking a rest, you might go out to get drinking water and in the dark there was little to see. But the next day, as you passed by the same place, you would see the many dead bodies all around. Also frightening was the story of

Mr. Itokazu being shot by a bullet yet not realizing until later, and the young lady being struck in the back by bomb fragments and dying the next day. Listening to these tragic war experiences, I feel pity and hopelessness for the situations people faced.

Mr. Itokazu mentioned that we should all treasure our parents. War seems to erupt all around the world, but in war, you only lose things. Mr. Itokazu's story will remain in my heart and we must make this world a better and more peaceful place. The story that I heard from Mr. Itokazu today will not be forgotten and I will try to engrave his story into my life.

Expressing My Gratitude for My Miraculous Survival during the War

Survivor: **Hatsuko Takayasu** Residing in Okinawa City / 89 years old
Interviewer: Sho Kinjyo   First Year in Senior High School
Interviewer: Miyu Hirose   First Year in Junior High School

Enjoying my work as a helper

The war was about to start when I was in 2nd Tomigusuku Normal Elementary School in 5th or 6th grade. In order to protect Okinawa many Japanese soldiers came to the islands. Japanese soldiers occupied large houses and schools in order to hide themselves and dug holes everywhere in the Okinawan mountains to create air raid shelters.

Constructing air raid shelters first required a framework made of pine tree wood to prevent the collapse of the soil in the tunnel. We upper-class students would help by peeling the bark off the pine trees and carrying soil outside as the Japanese soldiers dug the tunnel.

We students were not able to study at school at that time. Even now I can only write my name. It was that sort of age that we lived in.

I was born in the southern part of the main island in a farmhouse in Tomigusuku Village. We lived in a thatched roof house. Our family consisted of my father, mother, an older brother and sister, three younger brothers and our grandfather and grandmother.

In the old days, there was lots of housework for younger children. We would cut pieces of rush into thin strips, dry them and make straw mats. This was usually a job for women and girls and at night we would make the string required for the straw mats.

Sometimes housework could become a very unpleasant but it was an

enjoyable part of our life as well. I especially liked washing clothes and often went to the river where we washed clothes. Before the war, one of my greatest joys was helping out with housework.

In preparation for the war, our family dug a hole to the west side of our house to create an air raid shelter and for safekeeping of our food. I remember my grandmother cooking potatoes which we ate inside the air raid shelter.

This was the way it was before the war. I remember there was the strange sign of an odd star in the sky. I was able to see a long tail beneath the star - a comet. I recall an elderly lady with white hair telling us a story and she said, "If you can see a comet, this is an indication war is coming soon. This is a serious matter." She was saying that when a comet appears in the sky, it is a sign that something bad will happen. I still remember when she told us this story, worrying all us children.

Our family becomes separated in the war

Due to evacuation of the southern part of the island, it was around March 1945 when my mother took the younger children to Ogimi Village in the northern part of the main island. We woke up at four o'clock in the morning and loaded a wagon with various foods and sent them off at Naha station. It was sad to be separated from our mother but there was nothing we could do.

Instead of evacuating, my 13 and 5 year old brothers and I, 15 at the time, decided to stay at our house in Tomigusuku. My older brother, who was 17 years old, was called into the Japanese military. My grandmother was very concerned about my older brother.

My older brother escaped from his military unit and came home. He said, "We are losing the war and there is nothing we can do about it. I thought it would be better to escape, that is why I came home. At my military unit all we talked about was who died that day. No one came back from Shuri once they left here." My grandmother was so happy to see my

older brother and said while crying, "Now our whole family can escape here and I will have nothing to regret."

We stayed at an air raid shelter for a while but our whole family decided to flee since we were told that Shuri would be completely destroyed. When we looked back, we regretted that we had left the air raid shelter. Wherever we went, the entire island was a battlefield. But we thought we needed to escape, otherwise we wouldn't survive.

My father was carrying my 5 year old brother on his back, pulling my other young brother and me by the hand, while my older brother carried baggage on his back as our whole family evacuated further south.

At first our family went to Kanegusuku in Itoman City where my aunt lived. There was a strongly built air raid shelter but the shelter was not big enough for our entire family. Outside there was a hail of bullets everywhere. It would be too cruel for our aged grandparents to walk in such circumstances therefore we decided to leave both grandparents at my aunt's place. We decided to leave secretly and did not tell our grandparents. Those who were able to walk moved south to the area of Kyan Village.

I was told later that when we left Itoman City, our grandparents asked, "Where have our grandchildren went?" and they soon followed us south. There was little we could do about it but eventually, little by little, our family became separated in the war.

Trapped in the war, day after day

In Kyan Village at the southern tip of the main island, there was nearly no place for our whole family to hide in the local shelter. The place was overflowing with many Japanese soldiers, civilians and refugees, a large crowd of people like a festival. The U.S. bombing, mortar fire and bombardment by warships, pounded the Kyan area without mercy. Our family was inundated by waves of people trying desperately to escape.

At night we hid beneath the roots of trees to rest and during the day we

slept in a pigsty. My father and older brother brought wooden slats (which were used to carry the injured) from somewhere and placed them on the top of a hut and on top of that placed tree branches in order to camouflage from the enemy. I don't remember exactly how many days we stayed there but after about a week of bombardment from the sea and bullets from the sky, we were beside ourselves with fear.

Always thinking about where we could go to stay safe, our family was constantly moving. When we were hiding in the pigsty I was hit by a bullet fragment in my thigh. I felt something warm on my thigh and as I tried to brush it off, I found it was a bullet fragment. Others around me were hit in the head and shoulders but everyone in my family was strangely safe.

A young girl in my cousin's family cried constantly in fear. Worried that her crying might be heard outside our shelter, we kept a cloth in her mouth at all times.

There was no food anywhere, so we went to the sugarcane field and chewed sugarcane. We would sprinkle sugar onto beans and eat it as a sweet treat. Just before my father's cousin passed away we made a hot drink from sweet potato cooked in water and give it to him to drink. This was the least we could do before he died.

My older brother helped to pump water from the well. Surrounding the well were many black corpses swollen like balloons. In those days when I saw dead corpses piled up one after another I didn't feel fear. What I feared most was dying myself. Really, I did not feel like a living person. Strangely, if there was a crowd of people gathering then I felt somewhat safe. My father had chronic kidney disease and often he was breathing hard and seemed to be in pain, however, he told us, "Don't worry; I will be fine," and he encouraged us children.

Seeing an American soldier for the first time

Our family was driven further south and reached the precipitous cliffs

of Kyan Cape. The sea was in front of us and there was no place for us to escape. I was thinking that we should all jump from the cliff to our death but I was afraid of dying so we decided to hide in a growth of brush under a nearby pandanus tree. Even though I was stuck by the thorny leaves of the pandanus tree, I didn't feel much pain. Our family bunched tightly together and hid inside the thick growth beneath the tree.

The rain poured down hard all night while machine gun bullets were flying all around. Some bullets missed me by inches causing dirt to spray all over my body. I managed to persevere by covering my ears and eyes while remaining beneath the tree. I wasn't sure how much time passed before the surroundings became quiet. We were all looking at each other to see if each were still alive; everyone in the family showed their faces from the brush. Fortunately, we were all safe.

A soldier with a battle helmet came into the brush beneath the pandanus tree. At first, we thought a Japanese soldier had come to save us and we were all happy, but, when we looked closely we saw his nose was taller and his eyes were blue. It was first time for all of us to see an American soldier. The soldier was calling us by saying "Come out, come out." My father decided and said, "Let's go out," leading our whole family out from the brush. When we went outside my older brother was suspected of being a Japanese soldier and he was carefully searched by the American soldier.

Our whole family became prisoners of war. It rained all that day and an American soldier was carrying a newborn baby on his back. Then, he said to us, "Take this baby with you," and he entrusted the baby to us. However, we could not raise this baby under these circumstances and didn't know what would happen to us next so when the American soldier wasn't watching, we secretly left the baby by the side of the road. When I think about it now, I think we did a cruel thing but at the time we did not feel we had any other choice. In other places I had also seen children who had lost their parents following an unknown adult while crying and searching for their parents.

Our family was a truly rare example

Prisoners of war were all gathered together in the open square of a sugar refinery in Kyan. There were many injured people, some bleeding from their head, one with their arm torn off and even a person with a hole in their body. Even though I saw these gruesome scenes, I did not feel anything at all.

Our family was carried by a huge U.S. military truck to a field in Iraha Village in Tomigusuku. We were separated into groups of men, women and children and so my father and older brother were taken somewhere else. Thus our family became further separated from each other. As I stood near the chain-link fence I called out saying, "Father! Father!" but there was no response from my father. I cried all night thinking that I would never again be able to live together with my parents.

As soon as we became prisoners of war my older brother was taken to Hawaii. My father was taken to the northern part of the island to Ginoza. Later my younger brother and I were transferred from the Shimajiri (southern) area to the Ginoza concentration camp. There we were able to reunite with my father.

We were told by an acquaintance that my mother was also in the same concentration camp and my father searched her out and we were finally together again. When I saw my mother she was very skinny. One day when we went for a swim at the river, I was shocked to see her ribs stand out; you could count her ribs bones. She ended up just skin and bones. She told us that the evacuation place in the mountains of the far north of the island had been a great hardship for her and she looked careworn.

After that our whole family went back to our local community in the south. At Tomigusuku we cultivated a field together and grew potatoes and such. We also received regular distributions of canned foods from the U.S. military but that by itself was not enough for us to support our entire family.

Since the Shimajiri area was a place of fierce battle, entire families lost

their lives and there were many places where only the names on the houses were left. My grandparents, my parents, my father's older brother and his wife, and their younger brother and his wife - four households in all - were all safe.

Right after the war we were told that it was rare case for an entire family to be alive and safe. In the years after the war, together with our children we visited the camps for the prisoners of war. During the typhoon of steel our family was not blown away and during the war we were not seriously injured. It was truly a miracle that our entire family survived. I am sincerely grateful I have been able to live to nearly 90 years old.

The last thing that I want to say is that war should never again happen.

After the Interview ① **Sho Kinjyo**

I have listened to lectures on peace and visited the Peace Memorial Museum and learned about the war many times during my Elementary and Junior High School years. I have wanted to hear personal experiences of the war from my grandmother but she was only three or four years old during the war and she didn't seem to remember much. Hearing directly from someone who survived the war share her personal experience was very valuable to me.

Hatsuko Takayasu was younger than I am now when she experienced war. Living under such uncertain circumstances, never knowing when you might die and whether you would survive today or tomorrow, nevertheless, faced with this she kept trying and survived. I have come to realize how fortunate we are to live a comfortable life in a safe place in today's age, unlike those days of war.

Ms. Takayasu's expression looked very painful when she was sharing her personal war experience. Even though more than 70 years have passed, she still remembers very clearly about those times and will never forget those days. It made me realize how cruel and frightening war is. However, now Ms.

Takayasu lives a happy life and having seen a person who experienced such pain in the war becoming such a happy person also makes me very happy.

What is entrusted to us younger people in this day and age? It is to seriously learn, think and pass down to future people about this war. Lastly, I want to express my appreciation for allowing me to gain such a valuable experience. Thank you very much.

After the Interview ② **Miyu Hirose**

Until now I have read about the war and learned about the Battle of Okinawa through peace studies in school. However, I was very nervous this time to hear someone who had actually experienced the war directly.

When I met Ms. Takayasu she said with a gentle voice, "My talk is not such a great deal but thank you for coming to listen to what I have to say," and she softly touched my cheek. By listening to her, my tension was relieved and I almost felt like I was listening to my own grandmother.

Even now Ms. Takayasu still clearly remembers about the Okinawa battle and she told us in detail. The contents of her story cannot be imagined from her gentle, soft voice but it was a very frightening war experience.

People were hiding under the pandanus tree in order to conceal themselves from the enemy, they felt the heat coming from rifle bullets at their feet, surrounding them were many human corpses on the ground and even many of those alive suffered wounds on their bodies.

There were incidents of people taken by U.S. soldiers to the middle of a field in the night to be left behind and some young people were separated from their parents. I cannot imagine this happening to someone the same age as me and trying to put myself in this situation I became very frightened. After listening to Ms. Takayasu I have such a strong appreciation that I am alive today.

Until I listened to Ms. Takayasu's personal war experience I hadn't really thought about what is life, how to live your life and about the impact of the war. I now realize because my great-grandfather and great-grandmother

protected their lives, I exist right now.

Ms. Takayasu's family will be celebrating a newborn baby, her 13th great-grandchild, in March and I am so happy to see this happen.

I have learned so much from Ms. Takayasu's personal war experience. Though my family does not have its own war experience to share, I would like to pass down to my future family the story that I learned from Ms. Takayasu. In order to do so I first would like to challenge myself with my daily studies and make efforts to achieve my goals one by one.

No Matter What Happens, War Must Never Happen Again

Survivor: **Jiro Yabiku** Residing in Naha City / 89 years old
Interviewer: Masaharu Nakazato Second Year in Senior High School
Interviewer: Marika Yoza Second Year in Junior High School

Though I attended school we only labored for the war effort

My hometown is Mawashi Village in Uema (part of present day Naha City). Uema is a high, hilly area and at the time was a peaceful farm village. I was born in a place called Yabikuguwa in Mawashi and my family consisted of my grandparents, my parents, my grandfather's sister, an older sister, three older brothers and a younger sister who passed away when I was young.

Up until I graduated from Mawashi Elementary School our lives were routine.

During summer break of my 6th grade, our school was occupied by Japanese soldiers. The soldiers used our classrooms and we students conducted our school lessons under the big banyan tree in the schoolyard. Our graduation ceremony also took place under that banyan tree.

Upon entering junior high school, although we went to school, manual labor was assigned from morning to night and not once did we read a textbook.

One day our teacher instructed us to bring our lunch and a hammer to school the next day and so we did. Our teacher then told us that starting today we are all going to work. We students sang military songs, something like "we will bravely win the war." Walking for more than an hour, past Nichumae, past Gajyanbira in Oroku, we came upon the area called

Kakinohana. There, Japanese soldiers brought large bags and instructed us to work in groups of five and collect stones in the bags. The soldiers would mix the stones with cement to construct foundations for cannons. As we filled the bags, soldiers came and collected them. There were thirty to forty men building an entrenched position.

On October 10th, 1944, an air raid destroyed Naha harbor and the airport. By afternoon from Uema hill we could see the entire city of Naha was burning.

To take shelter from the air raid, we opened tombs and crawled inside. Eventually Uema became a fortified position for the Japanese military including a big shelter near Shikina Garden, which served as a field hospital. My grandfather offered a house on high land to the Japanese military to use as a firing position. After the air raid we were not sent to Oroku again and instead we helped the Japanese soldiers dig shelters in our local community.

In my first year of high school, the military was recruiting soldiers from the school and three of my classmates applied. At school I saw some students setting up a straw dummy to practice stabbing it with a bamboo spear. Once, a small tank came through Uema and when I saw seventeen or eighteen-year-old boys looking so cool in their uniforms, I too longed to join the military. Without telling my parents, I submitted my application but I was not called to service. At that time, it was considered an honor if you died in the war and I was not afraid of dying. Later though, others who applied together with me told stories about soldiers carrying bombs who would jump into enemy tanks, sacrificing themselves. War is about killing other human beings. When I think about it now, this is utterly foolish.

Trying every day to escape from the air raids

The air raids on Okinawa started on March 23rd. It was the morning of my school graduation day. From that point, the air raid bombing continued

every day. Our graduation ceremony was never held and even until today, I never received my diploma.

Once the air raids began, to stay safe at night we would close all the doors so light would not leak out. Since Uema is located on a hill, we could see the ocean. If light would shine outside it was seen by the enemy and we would immediately become targets for bombardment from the warships.

One day when we were inside our shelter, Japanese soldiers from the Stone Unit (the common name of the Army's 62nd Division) came in and said, "Starting tomorrow the Stone Unit will be using this shelter so you will all need to leave," and "Anyone remaining here will be considered a spy." Anyone thought to be a spy would be killed. Left with no choice, we immediately prepared to leave the safety of the shelter though it was very cruel.

When the bombing slowed at dusk, we fled with a group that included forty to fifty elderly women. We gathered our baggage and food and left the shelter. We walked through the night, reaching a place called Funakoshi in Tamagusuku Village (present day Nanjo City) at about five o'clock in the morning. We first tried to shelter in the cover of a rocky outcrop but it was raining and we thought this would be really hard on the elderly so we went to Fusato and there we decided to rest in the empty houses in the neighborhood as the owners had all evacuated elsewhere.

As we were resting in the abandoned houses, we came under attack by bombardment from the American warships. My grandmother, my nephew, my aunt and her three children, another aunt and uncle and their seven children, and a great many people from the village were killed by the bombs. Those of us who survived moved further south on the island.

Walking from Fusato for about two days, we came to Arakaki Village in the Shimajiri District. Finding no shelter we cut the lower branches from a tree and hid under the tree. We stayed there for about a week and decided to set out for neighboring Kuniyoshi Village. As we approached Kuniyoshi we came upon several women crying and running from the area.

Several of the women were holding the hands of children as they walked towards us. They were all crying loudly. Later I was told a story that the U.S. military commander, Lieutenant General Butler, was killed in battle and as retaliation the Americans lined up the men of the village and killed them. My father told us it was time to go and he urged everyone to flee.

I remember the loud sound of crying babies in the village. Drawn to the place I found many people killed by the bomb blasts leaving no one alive there other than a few deserted babies. It seems very terrible, but in the intensity of war there was no time to think; you never knew when you might be next to die.

There was no hope to survive

At Arakaki, thirteen of the people fleeing together in our group died. Small reconnaissance aircraft scouted out positions and signaled the warships to target their bombardment. One day while sitting in a group, a bomb dropped among us. When we open our eyes, family members who were just in front of us had been blown away by the bomb blast. My mother suffered facial injuries and died. There was no time to shed tears. It was hard to dig a hole to bury her so my father simply covered her in dirt. And so we parted with my mother.

From there we moved south to Mabuni. Around that time U.S. military planes started dropping leaflets instructing Japanese to surrender. The leaflets said, "men will be killed" so it was decided the women and children would surrender first. As I was still a child, I went together with my sister to surrender. But when I saw the American soldiers I thought to myself that if I am going to die then I want to be with my father and we would die together. My sister called saying, "Come back," but abandoning hope, I returned to my father.

Only eight of us men were left there. We all went to the steep cliffs of Giza Banta and started climbing down. At the base of the cliff there were

many dead bodies piled up like a mountain. If you fell while descending you would end up covered by dead bodies. Looking upwards you would see those caught in the trees, hanging there dead. There were dead bodies everywhere. After people die their decaying bodies release a terrible smell but it seemed my five senses were paralyzed as I could not smell them.

My cousin had been injured at Arakaki and he was not able to walk. My father carried him on his back and descended down to the beach but he was exhausted. My cousin said to my father, "Don't worry about me. Just leave me here." We divided up some dried bonito and gave it my cousin as we said good-bye to him at the base of the rocks. He probably died there later.

The coral rocks were sharp and too painful to walk on in bare feet so we ripped off our own clothes and wrapped them around our feet as we walked along the shore. Meanwhile, the U.S. military called over their loudspeakers from their ships saying, "Come out immediately!" We thought we would be killed, so we continued to run from them. We had no hope of survival and all we could think was, when would we die?

Eventually we made it to Asato in Hanashiro Village. During the day we hid in a sugar cane field and nibbled on cane stalks like mice.

By night we made our way back to our own village. After walking for two or three days we reached Tomori. A Japanese soldier came from a field and said, "This place is too dangerous; you must be careful." We took to walking in a single-file line. A bomb went off making a "pop, pop" sound and then four people up front were shot by a machine gun. My uncle, who was in front of me, and some of the people behind me were killed by machine gun fire. Those of us who survived hid in the sugar cane field waiting for night to come but we were discovered by American soldiers. We all raised our hands and came out of the field. By then we were so exhausted and thought, they may as well shoot us if they want.

The American soldiers gave us provisions to eat. Each pack even included a sweet treat. We hadn't eaten for nearly a week so we ate every morsel. I still remember that meal so clearly; it was so delicious that I

cannot describe it in words.

Even now I wake up in the middle of night

Our village was completely burned down; not a single house was left. Only three of my family survived the war: my father, my older brother and me. Together with three prior soldiers, we formed a household of all men. We built a house, started our new lives, and immediately started planting the fields of a farm.

I was in charge of cooking and kitchen work. An older girl in the neighborhood taught me how to cook rice with slices of potato which we all really enjoyed. Sometimes to make a living we would steal blankets and towels from the U.S. military warehouse to trade for potatoes and rice.

During this time my father would often go to the southern part of island for two or three days at a time to search for my mother's remains. Eventually my father did find her and we were able to hold a memorial service for my mother.

Even now I still remember the war and wake up in the middle of night. Truthfully, I wanted to forget all about the war. But, when I think about building a peaceful world I know I must do what I can to tell everyone about the war. I want to proclaim loudly that no matter what, war must never happen again. This is my most fervent wish.

After the Interview ① Masaharu Nakazato

Honestly, before when I heard the word "war" the only thing that came to mind was what you see in a movie or on television. I might have felt it was frightening or I might have felt pity for the victims.

However, after hearing Mr. Yabiku's war experience directly, I came to realize that war is very real and it is much more cruel than I had imagined.

In the terrible conditions of war, most people could not take the time

to think about others as they didn't know what would happen in the next moment and they had little hope for survival. I realized that even if people were usually inclined to think and act for the sake of others, as they witnessed the horrible conditions of war, many of them would eventually lose much of their humanity.

It was considered a great honor if you died in war and were not afraid of dying. This was Mr. Yabiku's state of mind when he was still in junior high school. Nowadays, it is impossible to imagine such things.

Today, Japan is not involved in war and on into the future war must not again happen. For the future, we must explain the reality of war. This story I have heard must be passed down to future generations.

After the Interview ② **Marika Yoza**

There were two things I thought about after hearing this war story from Mr. Yabiku.

First, no matter how much time has passed, the brutal reality of war will never leave one's mind. I felt that maybe Mr. Yabiku was worried about frightening us and he wouldn't talk much about the tragedy of war. But, as I listened to the words of his story, I could imagine those days of misery and just the thought was frightening. I can really say that just hearing his story was painful and frightening. It is unimaginable what Mr. Yabiku lived through during the war.

War causes people to lose their humanity. I remember hearing this in our peace studies in school. However, our schoolteachers did not directly experience the war. Stories from war survivors like Mr. Yabiku are so valuable and they profoundly touch my heart.

The second point is how we should live from this point forward. It is now more than 70 years since the Battle of Okinawa and each year there are fewer and fewer survivors still with us. I believe we younger generations are now the important link.

It is up to my generation who may not know about war to pass the

"Heart of the Okinawan People" to the next generation. Each individual has a different view of the heart of the Okinawan people, but I feel the true, sincere heart of Okinawa can be heard in Mr. Yabiku's story. In spite of the fact that it was all he could do at the time to struggle for his own survival, he still remembered clearly the fate of those who died around him. If not for his concern, he would not have carried those memories with him from the past. Mr. Yabiku's great compassion can be seen by his thoughts about the people around him even though he lived through such horrible circumstances.

I really appreciate Mr. Yabiku for sharing his story with us and will never forget my gratitude. I want to earnestly share his experiences with future generations of youth. I must engrave in my being the true history of the tragedy of war as it happened in my birthplace of Okinawa and live my life with a sense of appreciation for the "ordinary circumstances" of my day-to-day life.

The Battle of Okinawa Where I Witnessed Hell on Earth

Survivor: **Sotoku Higa** Residing in Uruma City / 84 Years Old
Interviewer: Norito Miyazato First Year in Senior High School
Interviewer: Anju Asato Second Year in Junior High School
Interviewer: Shota Iwasaki First Year in Junior High School

Naha City was a lively place before the war

My parents came from Okinawa but I was told that both of them worked in a factory in Osaka, so after all that has come to pass, I don't know whether I was born in Okinawa or Osaka. I lost my entire family during the war so there was no one to pass on my family history. My earliest memories are of living on Okinawa. I was told that my father was a second lieutenant in the military, but he passed away a very long time ago so I don't remember his face.

My family lived in the Tsuji District of Naha City. In those days Tsuji was the center of Naha City and it was a lively business shopping district. There were three main streets called the "near" street, the "inside" street and the "back" street and there were lots of rickshaws waiting all over for customers under the shade of banyan trees. Big, magnificent-looking Japanese restaurants lined the streets in long rows. Two large department stores named Yamagataya and Maruyamago were also found there. Tsuji was also the home of the tower of Naha City Hall, a municipal hospital, a big bookstore, a large torii gate, a playhouse and the Arakaki bus line that used coal-burning buses. Naha City in the days before the war was lively and magnificent.

Near the harbor in Naminoue District there was a neighborhood called Okundakari where our family lived in a tile-roof house away from the lively

center of town. At that time our family consisted of four of us including my mother, my older sister, my younger sister and me. Besides our family there were others who lived together with us. An Okinawan folk song says, "only a very small amount can be earned in a day." Even though you worked hard all day, your wages were small and it was common for several people who earned a very small amount to stay together under one roof, helping each other out.

On the edge of a village, there was a steel tower called Sanmoji rising from a large rock near the ocean at Naminoue. Being small I would swim in the shallows. Tsuji town was surrounded by many traditional grave sites. The Naha City I remember from those days was completely burnt to ash during the coming October 10th air raid.

I attended Uenoyama National School. I wore a hand-sewn kimono that my mother made. Since I didn't have a belt I used a rope instead. It seems my mother considered what she had available and made an outfit that she thought would suit me. I didn't have shoes and went to school barefoot. Since I didn't have a carrying bag I used a large piece of cloth and wrapped up my notebook and pencil and tied them around my waist. Sometimes I would use a short pencil that my older sister had finished with by inserting it into a bamboo stick to make it long enough to hold. Our entire family was frugal and used everything until completely consumed.

I was a bit of a troublemaker. I wouldn't listen to anyone or accept advice; not even from my parents. I was always being scolded by my school teachers. I didn't study at all but instead chatted with other kids, climbed trees and behaved so badly at school I was often sent to the principal's office. I didn't have any friends either. I was teased for being poor and disliked by everyone. Most of the kids in Tsuji were children of wealthy merchants who came from outside of Okinawa Prefecture. Those kids wore nice clothes. There was also a lot of bullying at school. I was a lone wolf among the others.

The October 10th air raid attack in Naha

There was an air raid attack on October 10th in 1944. At the time, Japanese soldiers belonging to the Tama Military Unit (also known as the troops of the 32nd unit of Lieutenant General Mitsuru Ushijima) had created entrenched positions among the rocks in preparation for the coming land battle. The air was filled with fighter planes rushing forward. The Japanese military fired in response over and over, but the fighter planes continued to fly towards us one after another. Since the Japanese military only had limited ammunition, it was very clear that they were no match for winning the battle.

After the October 10th air raid our family escaped to my mother's hometown of Izumi in Motobu Village in the north of the main island. My mother sometimes carried me on her back as we traveled. Our mother took us to her home but almost immediately decided to take us all back to Naha. There had been no air raid attacks for a while and we thought the war would not come back to us.

In Tsuji there were lots of turtleback tombs. Since these Okinawan tombs are large, the Japanese soldiers had us use them as shelter when sleeping. We would take out the urns with ashes to empty the tombs. After the air raid, all the surroundings were burned and it was better to stay inside the tombs.

Old Okinawan tombs were also used by the Japanese military. Since they faced Naha Harbor looking directly out to sea, it was the best vantage point. My mother dedicated herself to making food for the Japanese soldiers and the leftover food was given to us children. This was how she was provided for us.

The air raid attacks by the American military again became fierce. At Naha Harbor, right in front of my house, it was especially intense. The bombardment from warships near the Kerama Islands was focused on Naha Harbor and formations of fighter planes flew directly overhead. As I watched this sight I was not frightened but somewhat mesmerized. It was

the horrible sight of the vicious attack. The Americans fired lots of bullets and our Japanese military returned fire. Both sides ferociously attacked the other. The Japanese military kept artillery shells inside the Okinawan tombs and I think there were twenty to thirty Japanese soldiers inside.

After the war, I heard that the best soldiers were in the Ta-ke Military Unit that was sent to Taiwan, while the soldiers left in Okinawa were not so capable.

In a moment, my entire family disappeared

One day a Japanese soldier with a military sword ordered us to evacuate, saying the U.S. military would soon land on Okinawa. I then realized the war was really returning. My mother decided we should move to Shuri where the Japanese military headquarters was located. My mother, my two sisters, and me evacuated.

Bombardment from the warships was very fierce with intense firepower striking us high and low. We were unable to stay in one place and moved about for almost one week. We didn't know what to do. If we were careless or exposed we would instantly come under fire from machine guns.

Until we came to Chinen in Tamagusuku, our entire family of four was together. One afternoon we returned from searching for food when a bomb landed in our hiding place. In an instant both soldiers and civilians disappeared. I looked everywhere for my mother and sisters who were there just moments ago, but they were gone. I realized they were all dead. My mother was dead and I lost my entire family; the intense emotion I felt cannot be expressed in words. I stood like a statue; no tears would come. From that point I was alone. My entire family was killed in the war.

In the end, I was not at all afraid. At that time I think my soul was dead. I witnessed many people killed right in front of me. Strangely I was never hit by the bullets. Being short was somewhat of an advantage for me. During the fighting I would fall on my stomach and walk like a crocodile. Watching many people meeting a very cruel death, I thought about the

best way to escape and protect myself. If I had walked upright, I probably would have been killed a long time ago.

Even alone, I continued to try to escape. I ate anything to survive. It would not be possible to survive if I didn't try something, anything. That is why I did things that normally no one would be able to do.

Wondering around in the battle field alone

When the sun went down, "star shells" (illumination flares) would fill the sky. When a star shell crossed the sky, the night became as bright as the day, forcing us to immediately hide. We couldn't find a hole or shelter so we would just dash into a potato or sugar cane field to hide. There was no one to tell you where you would be safe or when you should run so I was left to desperately protect my own life. We were told we might be killed if we were caught by the American military so we did anything to avoid capture. When you jumped into the fields you would find snakes, rats and other animals. Since we had no food I would catch snakes and rats to eat. I didn't care if anyone saw this and laughed at me. Honestly, I don't think there was anyone who cared.

Sometimes, when we were hiding, Japanese soldiers would come and tell us, "Go somewhere else!" or, "Get out!" If we didn't obey we would be killed straight away; it didn't matter if you were a child or an adult. The best hiding places were usually taken by the Japanese soldiers. Once I was ordered to leave a hiding place by the Japanese military and I did. Moments later it was bombed and destroyed. I felt then that whether you lived or died would be determined in the end by your destiny.

To escape, we went as far south as present day Himeyuri no To. It was there that a most fierce battle occurred. The U.S. military, Japanese soldiers and Okinawan people were thrown together in battle and many died.

If you tried to escape you were cut down by machine gun fire; the bullets came out of nowhere. There was no shelter to be found and all we could do was conceal ourselves under dead leaves in an empty sugar

cane field. We were under constant attack. Bombs exploded everywhere, blowing people to pieces.

Once a bomb landed nearby and I was buried in dirt thrown from the bomb blast. Though buried under heavy soil, I was somehow able to dig my way out and I fled to the coast. To survive I hid in a sugar cane field and desperately chewed on sugar cane. I heard an unfamiliar sound and when I turned to look I saw an American tank approaching. I had never seen that type of vehicle before then.

The U.S. military seemed to know civilians and Japanese soldiers were hiding in the fields. They would announce in Japanese, "The war is over; come out." However, we thought that if we were captured by the Americans we would be killed so we didn't come out from hiding. When we didn't surrender, the Americans used flamethrowers to burn the sugar cane field with a bright flame. People were running here and there and some people were burned to death.

I ran from the fighting and came to a shelter where about fifteen adults were hiding. Somehow I snuck into the shelter without any of the adults noticing me, but when I was discovered a man grabbed me by the neck and threw me outside. Maybe the Japanese military thought children would be a burden. Even though they told me to go somewhere else, there was no place to go so I was just stood there silently. Although they didn't want me in the shelter, the battle was so fierce I forced my way in. In order to survive, I really didn't care what they might do to me.

The cruel and gruesome reality of war

During battle, some people seemed to lose their minds. I saw one Japanese soldier tear off his military uniform and rip off the clothes of a dead Okinawan man to disguise himself as a civilian. But, since he was a soldier he kept his gun and hand grenade for protection. It didn't seem he had any intention of surrendering to the Americans. Inside the shelter the Japanese soldiers told us they would kill us if we took even one step outside. We

were all very frightened of the Japanese soldiers and mostly stayed still but some people were unable to bear the intense stress and tried to escape. They were shot and killed right before my eyes. There was nothing we could do about it; we were helpless. Since there was no place to bury the dead, we left their bodies in the shelter for almost a week.

Great numbers of people lay dead in the field outside but there was no smell. We couldn't take a bath and were filthy so we all must have smelled really badly, but somehow we couldn't tell. The situation probably paralyzed our sense of smell.

Using a stick I caught and ate a snake and a centipede. There were seed potatoes planted in the field and I ate that too. My best treat was a frog; I ripped off the legs and ate every part of the frog raw.

I also drank my own urine. I found a rusty can and even without rinsing it I saved my urine in the can and drank it. By that time I didn't have any feelings of hunger and the only thing that came to my mind was a fear of when I would die.

Out in the field I would go through the dead people's pockets one after another searching for food. I found sugar and little hard, dry biscuits which I ate to survive. I also saw many starving children. Most of these kids' mothers were dead though they had survived. But there was little we could do to help these children. If we tried to help them then we would become the starving children. In the end we even stole from each other.

Inside the shelter I saw Okinawan civilians choking a Japanese soldier to death while he was sleeping. The Japanese soldiers threatened the Okinawans and were a grave danger to our very existence. In order to survive, Okinawans were forced to resort to actions like these.

Once I saw a group of school teachers and students attempt suicide by using a hand grenade. They pulled the pin from the hand grenade but it failed to explode.

After the war, I had a chance to see a television show of the Battle of Okinawa but what I experienced in the war was completely different from what was depicted. What I experienced was much more cruel and

gruesome.

Escape continues and life after surviving the war

No matter what, I was determined to escape. Once I went to the American soldiers' encampment and climbed into a U.S. military truck with other kids about my age. They took us to a prisoner camp where all the war orphans seemed to be gathered together. There were several dozen boys and girls there, all stripped naked without so much as underclothes. Upon seeing this I didn't want to be captured by the Americans, but the four of us were caught nonetheless. Even then, I didn't give up and while watching for my chance between the military patrols around the camp, I crawled under the fence on my stomach and ran away alone.

I had no one and there was no place for me to go. By then I was so tired of being on the run and my feelings were pulling me back to my mother's hometown. But it is almost impossible for a ten-year-old boy to make the journey all the way to Motobu Village in the north.

When I escaped to Ginoza Village I found many refugees were living in a thatched-roof building they had constructed. Seeing so many Okinawan civilians there, I decided the U.S. military would not kill Okinawans for no reason. In my heart I held out hope that someone would help me. In a simple child-like manner I had a strong determination to survive.

Due to such a long time without proper nutrition, my abdomen was swollen. Somehow I managed to survive by drinking water from a river. I wore an American military jacket but had no pants; the jacket extended down to my feet so the lack of pants wasn't a problem.

I found a batch of cooked potatoes in the yard of a farmhouse in Ginoza. I started eating them and put some in my pocket. As I was becoming full, a man discovered me. He yelled, "Go home!" and hit me with a stick. But I was so exhausted and didn't want to run anymore and anyway, there was no home for me to go to. After a moment the owner of farmhouse seemed to understand my situation and he relented, having decided I could stay in

his house. He said to me, "If you work in support of our family, I will raise you just like my own son. Do your best, okay?" I think he let me stay at his house because he needed laborers in the field. I didn't have any place to go so I quickly agreed.

The house owner's wife came to love me and she really did take care of me as if I were her own son. Living together as part of this family, I felt my humanity return and my life changed. Eventually my emotions returned and I felt like my soul came back to life. This family was truly my savior and I owe them my life. Even now during every Obon and New Year's celebration, I visit the Matsuda neighborhood of Ginoza Village to pay my great respect to the Yasumura family.

After the war I worked as a firefighter in Ishikawa for 30 years. At first I thought I would be all alone in this world but I met my wonderful wife and my life changed completely. Today I am surrounded by two sons and seven grandchildren. My goal is to live to the age of 100.

I have faced things that most people normally do not experience in their lives. Somehow I had the good fortune to survive the war. I also overcame being orphaned by the war and am alive still today. Even now I can't say why I had such a determination to live through the war. I just know I wanted to live so desperately; perhaps it was just basic instinct. Having lived through the hell on earth of the Battle of Okinawa, I am utterly against war under any circumstances.

After the Interview ① **Norito Miyazato**

On March 23rd, 2019, Mr. Higa shared his war experience with us three junior and senior high school students. Mr. Higa said, "War was such an extreme situation and I felt my soul was dead." His parents and sisters were all killed during the war and he had no one to rely on in order to survive during his time alone as a refugee. He is truly a remarkable person.

If I was in his position with no parents or siblings or friends, I would

probably lose the desire to live and just give up on living.

After hearing Mr. Higa's story, I thought to myself that from this point forward, we must never start another war. War itself does not produce anything. Whether winner or loser, no one benefits from war. Those who start a war are foolish. The first point of history should be to ensure we never forget the consequences of war.

After the Interview ② **Anjyu Asato**

As I heard the story of the Battle of Okinawa from Mr. Sotoku Higa, the first thing that came to my mind was the word "cruel." There were three main reasons for this.

First was the change to the environment. Until he was 10 years old, Mr. Higa was living an ordinary, happy life when suddenly, the war began and his homeland became a battlefield.

Second, it was the lack of food. I understood that during war there would be much less food to eat, but I couldn't know that Mr. Higa had to eat frogs and insects to survive.

Finally it was when he said, "his soul was dead." I asked him what was the most painful situation he had faced during the war. Mr. Higa said, "There was nothing left inside me. Since my soul was already dead, even when my family was killed I didn't cry. Even when I saw dead bodies I didn't feel anything." I thought to myself that war even robs a human being of their heart.

War should never happen. To help prevent future wars we must pass these war experiences to posterity so people in the future inherit a true understanding of the cruelty of war.

After the Interview ③ **Shota Iwasaki**

I had a basic understanding of the effects of war upon the people through television programs and lessons in school, but this was the first time I had

the opportunity to hear the details of one individual's war story and I came to understand more deeply the perspective of a war survivor.

It was very astonishing when Mr. Higa related how he lost all emotion and even though witnessing people dying right in front of him, he had no fear. It seems to me that an individual's normal mental state is lost when facing the possibility of death at any moment during a war.

Even just listening to stories about the war are frightening and it makes me think what would happen if we faced war again. Sufferings such as starvation and losing precious family members in war should never occur, but if the truth of war is not widely known, war may breakout again in the future. Having learned these things about war and having listened to such terrifying stories, I must spread this story widely to the next generation and ensure it is not forgotten as time passes. I truly hope we can rid this world of war.

Remembering My Older Brother Who Died in the War with Little Recognition of His Life

Survivor: **Den Nakamura** Residing in Yonabaru Town, Shimajiri-Gun / 88 years old

Interviewer: Yutaka Ishiki Second Year in Senior High School
Interviewer: Yuko Kuroki Second Year in Junior High School

My older brother was a hard worker and excelled at his job

The Battle of Okinawa took place when I was 13 years old and a first year student in the National Senior High School. The year I was born, 1931, was marked by the Manchurian Incident, beginning 15 years of war with the Republic of China which lasted until the end of World War II. The economy was bad and the era we lived in wasn't so good either.

In those days, boys who were 14 years or older were drafted into service as defense troops or "loyalty and courage" troops. My brother was the eldest of our siblings at 16 years old and was drafted into the loyalty and courage troop as a special attack soldier. Every time I talk about the war, the most painful thing for me is remembering my older brother.

Our family lived down the hill from Tamagusuku Castle which was in old Tamagusuku Village in the southern part of the main island (present day Tamagusuku, Nanjo City). The ocean at Hyakuna Beach was shallow to a considerable distance from the shore with truly beautiful blue waters. I spent many enjoyable hours swimming there.

My older brother's name was Denshin. I was second oldest at 13 years old. We also had younger siblings. My mother had poor eyesight and couldn't see far in the distance but was able to care for herself. When she was young,

she had served at Shuri Castle and always spoke in with formal, polite language. She styled her hair in a traditional Okinawan bun (Kanpu) and wore fashionable kimonos. We had no father at home and my older brother worked and supported our mother and family. While he was still in school he worked and fed our entire family. Tragically, he was forced to go to war and died. Every time I talk about the war I remember my older brother and shed tears. I truly feel sorry for him; because of the war my older brother did not enjoy his youthful days. He definitely sacrificed his life for us.

My older brother was often told that he was the hardest working person in the village. His work was difficult. I remember him complaining just once when I was in 5th or 6th grade about the difficulty of his work. When I was in 6th grade I did what I could to help him.

Even though my older brother was praised as the hardest worker in the village and excelled at his job, he still died in the war. Though he labored hard in the village, he was sent off to war. Sometimes these memories of my older brother come to me at night and I can't stop my tears.

Because of the deep emotions surfaced by these memories I have always avoided talking about the war.

Fear of bombardment from warships

In 1944, the Japanese army came to Tamagusuku Elementary School, where I had attended, and the entire school was taken over and became a garrison for the army. We turned to studying in an available office, but when the military took that too, we ended up not being able to study at all. Instead, we were forced to work all day long. Before long, my older brother was called into military service.

March 23, 1945, was the day of spring equinox. I remember our family cooked mochi rice (sticky rice) in celebration.

We heard the air raid siren and then planes buzzed back and forth. I was the oldest of the remaining kids in the house. Preparing for the attack, I released the livestock and let them go. Meanwhile, incendiary bombs fell

and set fire to the roof of our house. I couldn't extinguish it myself; there was nothing I could do about it. Our house was the first in the village to be burned. We crawled out and fled to a nearby shelter.

The next day bombardment from warships began. Our houses were destroyed by air raids and bombing and life in the shelter began. Even those whose houses remained could not go home because the battle was so intense. My family and I were assigned to a shelter in a place called Wachibaru. After a while, we were told that place was in danger, so we moved to a shelter called Tachiabu in Nakandakari District. You entered the bunker by descending a ladder.

How intense was the bombardment that Okinawa endured? They used a saying, "the bite of a ship's gun," to describe the fierceness of a ship's gunfire. The whole of Okinawa was bombarded by shelling from the warships. Many people died and those who survived were spared from the bite of the ship. When a large shell from a ship would strike, the ground was cleared leaving a hole nearly ten meters in diameter. When it rained, the hole filled with so much water that it was like a swimming pool.

There was a Japanese army camp at Kirabaru, the high ground of Tamagusuku. There were rumors that the U.S. military would land at Minatogawa in the southern part of the island, and all the artillery at Itokazu in Tamagusuku was aimed at Minatogawa and Ojima Island. I went to help man a cannon there. However, U.S. troops did not come ashore in the south. They pretended to unload tanks at Ojima Island at the south end of the main island, but turned and instead landed at the west coast of the central part of the island in Chatan and Yomitan Villages. The American military split Okinawa in two, with one contingent driving south to Shimajiri District and the other going north.

Even though we had evacuated to a bunker, we still were forced to work, even when there was shelling. When we were ordered outside to work, we were afraid of the bombs landing all around. Once a Japanese soldier yelled at fearful refugees, "What, you will not listen to orders!" as he drew his sword. Women, children and the elderly went in horror to work in the

surrounding encampment. We were forced to work on the encampment and dig shelters in the midst of the rain of steel.

Life as an evacuee in an underground shelter

There was a large underground bunker in Kirabaru in Tamagusuku Village, where the golf course is now located, and this natural bunker was overflowing with wounded soldiers brought south from Shuri. I went to help care for the wounded soldiers. The inside of the shelter was humid and felt like a sauna. The groans of pain made it seem like hell. I fanned a soldier suffering from gunshot wounds to the chest and waited for doctors and nurses to attend to him. Before long, blood began to pour out of the wounded soldier's chest with a gurgling sound and I fainted as I watched.

In the dark bunker it was hard to tell when night came. We even went to the toilet in the shelter. Since I don't go out, I lost my sense of time before long and my memory of those days is vague and empty.

In late May, the U.S. military came south from Yonabaru. It was pouring rain. An American soldier came to the entrance of the shelter and said, "Come out!" It had been drilled into us that it was better to die than to be held captive and humiliated. Almost no one exited because we had been taught that we would be killed if we were captured. However, a few people raised their hands over their heads and walked out.

I was hiding and watching this unfold. Suddenly, I saw my father leaving the shelter. My father had separated from my mother and lived separately and though he stayed in the same bunker, he never stayed with us.

Once, after the war was over, I asked my father, "Why didn't you ask me to come out with you when you left the bunker?" He said he had been told they would not kill prisoners of war if you put your hands up and walked out. However, if you spoke of this in the bunker, your entire family would be suspected of being spies against the Japanese military and you would be in danger of being executed. In those days, you might be killed by the Japanese military just for going out at night or for using the Okinawan

language. There were Japanese soldiers in the shelter, so my father didn't risk talking about these things then.

If we had known that we would not be killed if captured, we would have left with my father. But unaware of this, we ran from the battlefield and hid in the depths of the bunker and continued to suffer miserably.

As night fell, several families left the bunker carrying their packs on their backs. My mother, myself, my ten-year-old sister, my seven-year-old brother, and five of my cousins (my entire family), left the bunker and fled in the rain towards the south.

Trying to escape day after day with no place to go

My mother carried her pack on her head and I followed, carrying a bag of food and other items. With my mother's bad eyesight, she walked with me at a speed that was comfortable for all the kids as well. As we fled south we saw many decomposed bodies along the road. We kept walking through the downpour, getting muddy and resting alongside the road.

With a loud "bang," a shell blasted nearby, raining down dirt on my head and shoulders. If it was a bullet fragment instead, it would be all over; it would be the end of your life. After an explosion, you are in a daze for a while. After a few seconds of being unconscious, I'm remembered my family and called out their names. Grabbing each other's hands, we ran, trying not to get separated. I was thirteen years old and I was leading the family. But I had no place to lead them so I just followed after the other refugees.

Sometimes small groups of four to five people would go into a field to gather food and notice a landmine. In fields where the Japanese military had buried the mines, there was an abundance of vegetables since people would not venture there. I avoided the landmines and took the cabbage and carrots. I get nervous thinking about this, even now. It's wondrous I survived. There were many times when I was in danger, and many instances when I could have been killed.

While we were fleeing, my younger brother was injured in the leg by a

stray bullet. I tied the wound with a towel and my mother carried him on her back as we searched for a safe shelter. We found an air raid shelter dug into a bank and ducked into it. Families were hiding in another bunker nearby and I could hear the voices of children. After a while, a mortar attack began. Mortars are very dangerous because they land one after another in a long line, digging out a ditch. Artillery spreads more like a machine gun. The nearby bunker where the children's voices came from was totally destroyed. We felt unsafe there so we left in the night.

Families like ours with children were shunned by other refugees. After a search, we finally found a safe shelter with other refugees and Japanese soldiers in a dugout shelter. I remember a Japanese soldier saying, "Don't make a sound. Don't let the children cry." I heard a thump and smelled an intense odor as a shell was fired into the entrance of the shelter. Thinking it was poisonous gas, I put a cloth over my nose and mouth and endured the resulting pain in my throat and the difficulty breathing. We escaped from the bunker at night, but we were just wandering and didn't know where to go so I asked some soldiers. They told me the Japanese army was moving to Cape Kyan and civilians should go to Itoman. In the end, our family was on its own.

Frightened by the shadow of a U.S. soldier

It was a moonlit evening when suddenly, a figure came into view. There, right in front of me, stood an American soldier. Terrified, I threw the food I was holding and hid in the bushes. But as I looked more closely, it was just the long, stretched shadow of a U.S. soldier in the moonlight appearing as if he was nearby. My nerves were raw due to the constant state of crisis, leaving me sensitive to the slightest disturbance.

We had nothing; I lost our remaining food and there was no water. With nothing left to eat, I picked leaves from nearby trees and ate them.

We crawled out of the shelter on a moonlit night and climbed down the cliff. After a while, we were attacked by machine gun fire. We had wandered into an encampment without knowing it. As we were running away, a

bullet hit my mother's toe. I shouted at my family, "Don't move! Get down and don't move!" They all stayed still as I was directing the escape.

In the morning, our family crawled into a field to nibble on sugar cane. About that time, a U.S. soldier like a big, red demon, pointed a gun at me. I gave up; I had no other idea what to do. I didn't understand what the American soldiers were saying and they didn't understand our language either. They seemed to be telling me to go home, so I walked back to where my mother was. At that point, our entire family became prisoners and raised our hands above our heads. Amazingly, we had all survived.

Protecting our wounded family

My younger brother was wounded and his injuries were covered with maggots. I had tried to disinfect it with my urine but his condition was serious and he developed tetanus. My mother was also injured, so my family and I were forced to relocate from Itoman to a camp with a military hospital at Ginoza in the northern part of the main island.

Ginoza was facing a crisis; it was full of refugees and there was no food. We walked through the rice paddies and looked for sources of protein, such as frogs. But there were no frogs. There was not so much as a leaf left on the stalks. We survived mostly by eating a small amount of rationed rice. My sister was evacuated to Yanbaru in the northern part of the island, but she lost her child due to malnutrition because she could not produce breastmilk without food for herself.

There was a dump where they burned trash in Kushi Village (in present day Nago City). The U.S. military dumped their unwanted items there. When a truck would arrive to dump trash, several boys like me would run there as fast as we could to look for food. Sometimes we would find a big can of beef and say, "What a big treat!" We would happily carry it home and manage to stave off our hunger that day.

I was a junior high school student and in order to receive one rice ball in payment, I would to go to the field to trim trees and pick plants which

we would share among our family. At that time, my older brother had not returned from the war and we didn't know if he was alive or dead. It wasn't until we returned to our hometown that I learned of my older brother's fate.

My older brother had been killed in action. From the fifth or sixth grade, he worked so hard to feed my mother and his younger siblings until he was exhausted. I can't help thinking that he died a brutal death in the war at the young age of 16, without any repayment or recognition. I feel like crying when I think of my older brother. I wished for the happiness of my older brother because he struggled so hard in life and I can't help feeling sorry that he died because of the war.

I went with my brother's classmates to look for his remains. We found them at Gushichan in Yaese Town and were able to place his remains in a grave. I lost four male family members in the war and I don't know where most of them lost their lives.

In war, running away is not a bad thing

By 1946, we had returned to Tamagusuku Village. The first place we returned to was a temporary hut at Funakoshi in Tamagusuku, but we moved around for a while within the village. I was born and raised in the first district of Tamagusuku, but it became part of a U.S. military base so we continued to live in temporary housing.

I graduated from Tamagusuku Elementary Education in 1947. I didn't finish my sophomore year due to the war so I had to repeat that year again after the war. It took me four years to graduate from high school though the education system had changed to six years elementary school, three years middle school and three years high school. In those days I often wore clothing known as "HBT" after they were thrown out by the U.S. military. On the back of the clothes were painted "CIV" (civilian) and "PW" (prisoner of war). I wore an outfit with "CIV" on it. I didn't have a notebook, so I used a piece of paper rolled up into a tube.

The war killed some of Okinawa's best men and women. The students

in middle school and the Normal School were originally destined to be teachers in the future. Many lives were lost as a result of the war and there were few teachers after the war. Due to the lack of teachers, I was recommended to work at the school after graduating high school. While working at the school, I studied at Itoman Training School for six months and took courses in the summer to become a teacher. From that time forward, my life finally became stable. Since then, I have been working as an educator to make Okinawa a peaceful and prosperous place.

On the battlefield, it was all I could do to escape and find food to eat. I was desperate to protect my family. The only thing I could think about was fleeing from the dangers that faced us. I think that's why I survived. Running away is not a bad thing. Sometimes that is what is necessary to protect your life, regardless what others might order you to do. I heard of children who disobeyed their parents' orders, pretending to be dead in order to escape group suicide. The important part of education is to cultivate the ability to live.

In Okinawa, there is a word "nuchi-dou takara" (life itself is a treasure). Life is essential. No matter what happens, we must not go to war. Winning or losing a war doesn't change the fact that lives will be sacrificed.

After the Interview ① Yutaka Ishiki

Listening to Mr. Nakamura's war experience, I was strongly reminded once again that war must never be repeated. Mr. Nakamura lost his oldest brother, a very important family member, who worked very hard to support the family. As he related, even now when Mr. Nakamura talks about the war, he thinks of his older brother and he wants to cry.

I have never lost a family member, a loved one, or someone that supported me. It is easy to imagine that I would be overwhelmed by a sense of loss and despair that I wouldn't be able to put into words if someone important to me disappeared suddenly right before my eyes and I could

never see them again.

On top of that, Mr. Nakamura was forced to flee through a rain of bombs that might strike at any moment, without warning. I can't even imagine how horrible and painful it must have been for him.

Finally, Mr. Nakamura said, "Take a good look at yourself." He told us, "No matter how hard it is, take care of yourself." These words especially stuck with me. I'm sure I'll remember this throughout my life and I want to keep these words firmly in my heart.

I am grateful to Mr. Nakamura for giving me this opportunity to hear about his experience and I thank him for sharing his story despite the pain he faced in recalling these memories.

War takes the lives of many precious people and leaves nothing but sad and painful memories. War brings sacrifices to both sides, whether winner or loser. It has been deeply engraved in my heart that such a war must never happen again.

After the Interview ② **Yuko Kuroki**

Once more, I learned the horror of war. Until now, I had taken it for granted that my family would always be there for me. But I learned that war plunges your precious family and yourself into the horrors of death.

It is difficult to imagine that in Okinawa, where the war was so fierce that it was called a "rain of steel," that death was so close at hand. I don't think many people can imagine what Okinawa was like then compared to today's peaceful Okinawa.

I hadn't thought about it either. Listening to Mr. Nakamura's story made me think deeply, "What is peace?"

What is the meaning of the word "peace" and what supports peace? I think now it is the phrase "life itself is treasure" as stated by Mr. Nakamura.

Mr. Nakamura said, "No matter what happens, we must not start a war." He said, "Whether you win or lose the battle, it will cost you your people." We will take this message and baton from those who lived through the war and pass them on to the next generation.

Even after the War, Suffering Continues

Survivor: **Kojun Yokota**   Residing in Ginowan City / 84 years old
Interviewer: Miyuki Nakasone   Second Year in Senior High School
Interviewer: Hiroaki Haebara   Second Year in Junior High School

My recollections before the war

I have thought about taking my own life due to the great suffering I experienced due to the war. Even now I am suffering. If I encounter stress, even at work, I experience incontinence, sometimes even without me knowing it is happening. Regardless what I wear or where I sit, I soil my surroundings with urine. Once, I experienced extreme constipation and was unable to relieve myself for 20 days. Sometimes I feel I am losing my mind or control of my body.

I often need to remind myself that I am suffering from an almost incurable disease due to my experiences in the war.

Before the war broke out, our family lived in old Nishishin Town in Naha (present day Nishimachi, Naha). It was a lively business and shopping district and my grandmother managed a variety shop right next to the playhouse called Shinrakuza. Shinrakuza was a very popular theatrical company that attracted many visitors. Besides the theater, many visitors came to the area to buy kunpen (traditional Okinawan baked treat with a peanut paste filling) and tanna fakuru (traditional Okinawan hard biscuit made from cane sugar and flour) from our store which really prospered. The first thing each morning, I dusted off the front of the theater and helped my mother clean up. I remember riding the light railway to Yonabaru Village to buy sugar cane from a farmhouse.

I went to Uenoyama National School. My oldest brother went to war

and was eventually discharged from the military after the war. Just before the war broke out on Okinawa, my second oldest brother and younger sister evacuated to my mother's parents' house and my grandmother who was managing the variety shop evacuated to Katsuren Village to her parents' home. We housed four to five military messengers on the second floor of our house and as time went by there were an increasing number of Korean conscript soldiers in our town. The theater company's playhouse became a brothel for the soldiers and there were always many soldiers lined up there.

Terrifying air raid attack

Before daybreak on October 10th, 1944, I woke to the sounds of an air raid attack. The air raid started in earnest as I was eating breakfast. This was the beginning of the October 10th air raid. While holding a pair of chopsticks, I was seized with great fear.

The civil defense unit group leader called out saying, "Hurry and run!" and, "Go to your assigned tomb." A little after seven in the morning my grandfather, my mother, my younger sister Keiko and I ran inside a nearby tomb.

Behind the Shinrakuza Theater there were tombs used as air raid shelters. It was only five minutes walking distance and if you ran you could get there in two or three minutes. The tomb we went to was a large Okinawan-style tomb but once 30 to 40 people were inside, there was no longer any room to walk around. We had conducted evacuation exercises beforehand and already determined the fixed number of people assigned to each tomb.

After our family was inside the tomb, nature called and I really needed to go to the toilet. I asked for permission to go outside to urinate but the civil defense leader said, "If you go out now, we will be discovered by the enemy and a bomb will be dropped killing all of us." I had no choice but to hold it.

The sound of bombing was becoming ferocious and fire was getting very close to the front of tomb. Additionally the tomb was packed full of people. Between the heat coming from the people and the flames, I felt like I was half dead. At the time I thought this was how it was just before people would die.

I think it was around seven in the evening when the U.S. aircraft stopped coming and we were told we could come out from the shelter. I felt immense relief. The Shinrakuza Theater completely vanished during the air raid attack of October 10th.

That same year, two fine turtleback tombs built by my grandfather were destroyed in air raids. After the war, the land previously occupied by all these graves was confiscated by the U.S. military to use as a base and it was lost to us.

The air raid attack on October 10th forced our family to evacuate from Naha that same evening. My father led my mother, younger sister and I in a single file line as we walked barefoot for 14 hours until reaching Haebaru neighborhood in Katsuren Village (present day Uruma City). Katsuren was where my paternal grandmother's parents lived and since my grandmother was in weak health she had already evacuated to there earlier.

After entrusting me to my grandmother, my mother left together with my younger sister. My younger sister was only 3 years old at that time. At my father's family home in Haebaru there were many relatives and it was fairly safe, but my mother was worried that there weren't many people to support her parent's house in Nakagusuku Village. My mother felt she was needed to help and protect those staying at her parent's house so she hurried to Nakagusuku. She stayed at Katsuren for just one day.

My mother lost those she desperately wanted to protect

At the time of the air raid attack on October 10th, my father was working as a civilian employee of the Japanese military in a cycad factory in Ie Island. During the war they extracted starch from cycad plants and used

it as aircraft fuel. At the cycad factory in Ie Island, men who were drafted into military service also worked there.

When our family evacuated to Katsuren, our grandfather probably felt tremendous pressure from the responsibility of feeding the large number of children and he contacted my father asking him to figure out some way to come home. My father told the authorities his mother was in weak health and he was able to come to Katsuren where the entire family eagerly awaited him.

My father and I waited for my mother, brother and sister to return. After a while my mother took the family from Nakagusuku traveling to Katsuren on foot. In those days, Okinawa didn't have as many buildings and most of the roads were just mountain paths, so it was talking more time than she had expected. On her way to us in Katsuren, Chatan was attacked by the U.S. military and she was ordered to the Shimajiri District on the south end of the main island. She had no choice but to go there. Together with her mother and four children, she traveled through a fierce war zone at Mabuni Village on the south end of the island. She was forced to flee from one place to another, not knowing where to go to be safe.

During this U.S. military attack, my second oldest brother and younger sister died. My mother lost her children on the battlefield not knowing where to go to keep them safe. Through this, she carried her mother on her back trying to flee north to Kunigami Village, but along the way her mother died from severe malnutrition. My mother really wanted to protect her mother and children but lost them all.

Nearly one year after the war ended, my mother came back to Katsuren. She had a fragment of a bombshell still in her body. When we asked her what happened to my younger sister, her face turned pale and she couldn't speak. At that time, I came to realize that our family members had died. I didn't want to make my mother feel sad so we didn't talk about my younger sister and I didn't ask unnecessary questions about our family for a long time.

My younger sister Keiko had been 3 years old. The two of us were very

close. While fleeing the danger together with my mother at Shimajiri, she lost her life. My mother was desperately trying to save her dying child, running from place to place not knowing what to do. My mother later told me that just before Keiko passed away, she called my name, "Kojun, Kojun" several times. After hearing this I felt great sorrow.

Becoming a bridge between Okinawa and America

A middle-aged couple, cousins of my father, who had moved back to Okinawa from Hawaii also lived at our house in Katsuren. In Hawaii, the man had been a chauffeur for an American and the woman had been a housemaid of King Kamehameha. Being raised in Hawaii, their food, language and culture were all Hawaiian. They both had done well financially in Hawaii and when they came to Tomari in Naha, they opened a hardware store. However, they were chased out by the war and came to live at our parent's house in Katsuren. They both worked as an interpreters for the U.S. military.

After the war, Okinawa was separated from mainland Japan. We lived under the rule of U.S. military administration and Japanese currency was not accepted in public. Those who were able to speak English and work as an interpreter were given very favorable treatment. Instead of paying us in money, American soldiers provided canned food and snacks brought by truck. We stored the provisions in our basement and distributed them to our relatives. I often saw the couple from Hawaii laughing and engaged in happy conversation with the U.S. soldiers. Since schools had not yet reopened, they taught me multiplication, and when American military officers came to our house, I sat with them during their visits, soaking up the conversation.

When we were living in Katsuren I saw ten to twenty trucks in a line passing by our house. I was told by my father's cousin from Hawaii, working then as an English interpreter, that the corpses of the war dead were being carried to White Beach and from there, they were loaded on

ships to be thrown out to sea. I stood without moving in disbelief of this tragic scene.

After the war I had the opportunity to live with someone who had lived overseas and from them I was able pick up English which greatly improved my situation. By the time I was in senior high school, I had mastered enough English to serve as the interpreter for our school principal.

After high school I went to International University (present day Okinawa International University) as a member of the first class of graduates. As time passed, my dreams for the future included strengthening the ties of friendship between Okinawa and America. At one time I worked as an interpreter for the U.S. Military Commander of Futenma Air Station and I strived for friendly relations between the Ryukyu Islands and the United States. Later I became interpreter for the Ginowan City Mayor. My life after the war fully involved both the U.S. military and Okinawan residents.

Since the war, I have suffered greatly from medical conditions regarding urination and constipation. Continuing today, ever since the air raid attack on October 10th, I have suffered greatly from urinary incontinence and frequent urination. This affliction stays with me even more than 74 years after the war.

I have had no peace of mind but even today I am determined that the Okinawan people will not again become victims of war. This is the conviction that I carry throughout my life.

After the Interview **Hiroaki Haebara**

Upon hearing the war experience from Mr. Kojun Yokota, I have come to realize and understand how frightening war really is.

From the start of the air raid attack on October 10th, great numbers of people were killed with no distinction between whether they were military or civilian. The effects of such indiscriminate bombing left a strong impression

on me. Hearing the loud sound of the air raid siren, Mr. Yokota, who was just starting breakfast, became so frightened that he fled while carrying chopsticks in his hand. Sheltering in a nearby tomb, he was unable to go out to relieve himself and had to hold it in for eight long hours. It must have been really difficult for the 10-year-old Mr. Yokota to endure this agony.

Even during the calm between attacks Mr. Yokota was unable to sleep well due to incontinence which continues even until today. I was very surprised to learn that people continued to suffer in this way even after the war.

After the war Mr. Yokota diligently studied English and for about ten years he worked as an interpreter on the U.S. military base. I was impressed by how he strived in taking various actions for the cause of peace between Japan and the entire world.

From this point I think it is very important for each of us to become a center for peace in the world. In order to create a peaceful world it is important for us to value the people who are close to us and we must teach the next generation about war and why war should never again take place.

I Will Never Forget the War That Took My Beloved Older Brother's Life

Survivor: **Fujiko Miyagi**   Residing in Okinawa City / 92 years old
Interviewer: Maria Funauki   First Year in Senior High School
Interviewer: Hisui Funauki   First Year in Junior High School

Standing guard, cane sugar, and bamboo spear training

I was born in 1928 in Kayo, Kushi Village (present day Kayo in Nago City). My seven-member family consisted of my parents, three older brothers, a younger sister and me.

I loved to study and never missed a day of school. I was a good runner and I was the starter position for relay races. In junior high school I played volleyball. When I was thirteen years old there was a big tournament at the school. We were defeated two games to one by the junior high school team from Ie Island. I still remember it well. Our house was on the oceanfront so when I had time after coming home from school I would go swimming in the ocean. This is how I spent my days.

One of our preparations for war at the village was known as "standing guard." We would take turns climbing up a tall tree to watch for the enemy. If you saw enemy aircraft you were to shout loudly to alert the whole village, "Enemy plane approaching, prepare for attack!" Otherwise, we would go to the farm near the beach to dig up potatoes.

In those days, what I liked most was cane sugar. There was a brown sugar factory near our house with bundles of sugar cane stalks all lined up. The factory made cane sugar using a machine to squeeze juice from sugar cane. Then it was put into tins and placed on the roof where children could not easily reach. Though it was wrong, we would post someone to watch

at the front of the house and then climb up to the roof to take some of the cane sugar to eat.

One of the lessons at school was bamboo-spear training. We would go to the mountainside to find straight bamboo and make a spear by sharpen one end. We would practice our guard phrase, "Enemy plane approaching, prepare for attack!" and stab with the spear. We did this every day for one hour. Once, when my older brother went to gather bamboo, he was bitten by a snake.

Working to prepare for war and the time in between

I also helped with war preparations under order from the Japanese military. My father and I went to Ie Island to help build an airfield. We tied a Japanese headband on our forehead and headed towards the harbor. From there we were taken to Ie by boat. Once we arrived at Ie we walked to the airfield. There, the work of beating the ground with a log was awaiting us. We worked in groups of two to harden the runway. We were not told that this was in preparation for the war, but it was. On Ie Island, the Japanese soldiers ate delicious potatoes while the Okinawan civilians were forced to eat potatoes infested with insects.

I made a friend on Ie Island and we exchanged letters. Her name was Sumiko and I got to know her through volleyball. We both played setter position and we soon became very good friends. When I wasn't on Ie Island we exchanged letters between Kayo and Ie. She was quite tall. I usually talked about volleyball in the letters. We promised each other to be friends forever.

When I went to Ie Island to work we would meet. We talked about the war, how it was frightening and how might we prevent the coming of the war. I really liked Sumiko and I wanted to always stay in touch with her. I remember eating potatoes together nearby a family tomb. The potatoes were infested with insects but we picked then out and ate the potatoes. This is a good memory and it was a great treasure for both of us: spending

time together with a good friend.

Sumiko came to visit me at Kayo after the war broke out and I provided potatoes and rice for her to take back.

Once the work was completed at the airfield and we returned to the main island, there were Japanese troops everywhere and there were no trucks available to take us, so we walked all the way home.

Visiting my older brother who was drafted into Japanese military service

Low-altitude aircraft bombed Okinawa during the October 10th air raid. The vendor stands in the center of the village and five or six houses burned down. All the cows and pigs were killed so we decided to share the meat for eating. Two ladies visiting from Nakagusuku died at that time as well. A terribly awful smell comes from dead bodies. We heard that enemy soldiers had come to the nearby village of Teniya and several people had died. When it was safe there, we buried the dead.

Once the air raid started, our entire family evacuated into the mountainside. At that time my older brother was called up for military service. While living in the mountains, I made a soldier's good-luck belt with a thousand stitches embroidered by a thousand different women but before I could finish, he went into battle at the age of 20. He was drafted into the 24th Division also known the Yama Military Unit.

I was so worried about my beloved older brother. I learned that he was stationed at Yomitan and since my uncle came from Yomitan and served as a guide for the military, I was able to pass through the mountains and visit my brother at their entrenched position. Since I was good at sports and in good physical shape, the journey wasn't difficult. Even while walking alone I was not afraid. My brother told me that if the Americans did not come to Okinawa soon he may be sent to Hokkaido to fight against the Soviet Union. Crying, I told him, Okinawa is already in the war and I begged him not to go to Hokkaido. Trying to comfort me, my brother said there is

nothing we can do if the military ordered him to go. I went twice to see my brother in Yomitan.

My brother's military unit was transferred from Yomitan to Shimajiri District in the south. I also went to see him at Shimajiri. I traveled through Kin Village, to Naha and then went further south. My aunt lived in Oroku, Naha and I stayed overnight at her house on the way. It took me three days to get to Itoman Village to see my brother. I braved the journey alone to make sure my brother was alright. When I arrived at the encampment in Itoman, I asked for Adaniya, our Okinawan family name. Okinawan names were not familiar to the Japanese soldiers and I had to correct them over and over saying, no, it is Adaniya. I had come all the way to Itoman and I was desperate to see my brother. Finally my brother emerged from the shelter to see me. I gave him cane sugar that I brought caringly from home. This was last time I saw my brother.

No word of my older brother for a very long time

We didn't know for a very long time when my beloved older brother had died. We were told that he had decided to stay at the air raid shelter in Itoman and died there. We also heard only two people from his company survived and they had gathered his remains and held a memorial service after burying him. We created a memorial tablet with the name of my older brother first and my father's name beneath his: Adaniya Churo (my brother) – Adaniya Chuzo (my father). It was many years before his remains came back to our family. In 1988 we were able to find where he had been buried and recovered his remains. More than 40 years had passed since the war. Although our family didn't know when he died, once we had found his remains we finally felt that he had truly been killed in the war.

Back home at Kayo, our exile in the mountainside continued. My father was together with our family. My father was still young at the time, but because he was short in stature he was excluded from military service. However, he was a very hard working person. My father taught me many

things during our mountain exile for example, putting unpolished rice into a 2 liter bottle and using a bamboo stick to clean the rice.

Coming from the direction of neighboring Higashi Village, we could hear the loud sound of American soldiers marching. As soon as we would hear their footsteps we would hide in the mountainside. One rainy day we were hiding under an outcropping of rocks when the rocks and dirt broke free, burying us. Since I was wearing a hat and it allowed me to breathe, I was safe. Sometimes my cousin and I would hide under ginkgo trees. We thought we were well-hid, but although our heads were covered, our lower body was still visible. We saw each other and both laughed.

When we were finally taken prisoner, my grandmother tied a white towel to a bamboo pole as a flag of surrender and we came down from the mountain.

There is nothing more terrifying than war

The war ended when I was 18 years old. I had worn my long hair braided but I cut it. We were told that if you were seen by American soldiers they would treat you very cruelly. I was truly scared and even at home I would hide inside the wardrobe and the cabinet under the Buddhist altar.

One day my father told me I had been assigned to wash American soldier's uniforms and not to take this lightly. It was hard work they wanted someone else to do as lots of insects were ground into their uniforms. The soldiers brought their dirty clothes in bags. Since I didn't want to wash their clothes I tried ignoring them and would not listen to them. Then one time they brought lots of cigarettes and sweets for me.

The soldiers brought a big scrub brush and bars of soap. They gestured, showing us how to wash and said, "You wash, wash, okay?" and "This soap is not for you to eat, this is for washing." Even now I still remember our simple conversations with the American soldiers.

During the war it was very terrifying. We were using spears made from trees and the American soldiers were using machine guns and pistols. So

many people died. I always remember even today about the war. It is grave mistake to think that war is a gallant sword fight. We must truly understand that war is a life and death situation for actual people. There is nothing more frightening than war; there is nothing more terrifying.

After the Interview ① Maria Funauki

Watching Ms. Fujiko nearly in tears while recalling her memories of the war, I could tell she must have been truly frightened during the war and her emotions really touched my heart.

If I had been in Ms. Fujiko's place, I don't know if I could have endured the circumstances of war.

We should never again allow war to occur. It was good that I came to realize through her war story that there is nothing more frightening and terrifying than war.

Recently I had a chance to travel outside of Okinawa Prefecture and meet with others of Ms. Fujiko's generation. I was quite surprised as they said that since Okinawa suffered the hardships of war, they didn't have to. It almost sounded like the war in Okinawa was of no concern to them. They had been able to attend school when the Battle of Okinawa was raging. They said they had no experience of war on the ground.

Every year there are fewer and fewer war survivors still with us. I feel that junior and senior high school students outside of Okinawa have almost no opportunity to hear firsthand experiences of the war. Those of us born and raised in Okinawa have a mission to tell others about what happened here and to pass these stories on to the next generation.

To build a peaceful future it is important for Americans, Japanese and people of other countries to come together as equals with no discrimination.

I want people not only in Japan but across the entire world to understand we must never repeat war and that there is nothing more frightening and terrifying than war.

After the Interview ② **Hisui Funauki**

Hearing the talk from Ms. Fujiko, I think she is really a brave person. During the war, Ms. Fujiko was about the same age I am now. I don't think many young kids today would have been able to do what she did, taking care of her sick younger sister and traveling long distances to see her older brother. I really think she was both mentally and physically strong.

While telling her story, she repeatedly said there is nothing more frightening than war. In school we have previously learned about the war. I have had the chance to hear war stories from survivors but this is the first time I heard the details of their daily survival, how they hid and how they escaped. Hearing her thoughts and emotions as she describe each scene, I felt like I was there.

I now feel strongly that there is nothing more frightening than war. Hearing this story of Ms. Fujiko's own experiences has been a great benefit for me.

I want to become a person able to explain to others people how frightening war is and that we should not take our current peaceful existence for granted. Rather, we need to appreciate each day, enjoying what there is to enjoy, and spending our lives each day to create value.

All I Want Is To Erase the Memory of My Nineteenth Year

Survivor: **Tsuru Yonamine** Residing in Kunigami-Gun, Nakijin Village / 94 years old

Interviewer: Mizuki Yonaha Second Year in Junior High School

The last students taking the physical examination for conscription into military service

I was born in the Heshiki neighborhood of Nakijin Village in the northern area of the main island. Our family was known to be exceptional farmers and we were wealthy enough to hire a housemaid. I was an only child. When I entered elementary school my father taught me mathematics. Although I was not good at math at first, because my father tutored me each day and had me write out problems using an ink block and brush, I improved. Even though it was my mother's second marriage and I was not his biological daughter, my father really loved me and raised me as his own. I am filled with a deep sense of appreciation towards my father.

Nakijin Normal Elementary School was located in present day Nakaharababa. It was located in a mountain village in the north of the island and there were about forty students. About thirty students were able to go on to junior high school.

Students of our grade level and higher were eligible for conscription into military service and underwent the required physical examination. Our classmates were among the last to be enlisted and we thought we were very unfortunate. Women were not drafted into the army but our male classmates were forced to go to war and many of them died.

After graduating from the junior high school, I went to Ooita Prefecture

to work at a silk mill on a three-year contract. My mother was a great support since my parents raised silkworms at home. Four or five of my friends from the area went together.

After two years in Ooita Prefecture I received a letter from my father asking me to come home. However, I couldn't since my contract was for three years. So, my father sent a letter to the company saying untruthfully that, "My daughter is getting married," which forced me to return home. I came alone back to my hometown of Nakijin, separated from my friends in Ooita Prefecture. I was eighteen years old at the time.

Fleeing every day through the air raid attack

On October 10, 1944 came the first air raid attack. As I recall, this was the beginning of the Battle of Okinawa.

Earlier that year my father was mobilized by the Japanese military and was sent to Ie Island for maintenance work at the air field. The notice would come directly to your house back then and when you received this notice it didn't matter how busy you were, you had to follow the order and report. By October, Okinawa was becoming chilly. We received a message from my father asking for us to bring him warm clothes and a blanket. He also said the food was not so good so please make him some of the sweet soybean paste called abura miso.

I was asked to take everything to my father on Ie Island. As my mother was making the abura miso the night before I was set to leave, two ladies who had heard I was going to Ie Island came to see us. They said they had family living on Ie and they wanted to accompany me.

We woke up early and headed towards the harbor in Toguchi at Motobu Town in order to make the nine o'clock ferry in the morning.

We walked for about ten kilometers and just as we came down the hill into the Jahana neighborhood in Motobu Town, we saw an aircraft flying towards us. We all thought it was a Japanese military aircraft and we enthusiastically cheered. However, a member of the civil defense unit

riding a bicycle through the village was shouting, "An American aircraft is approaching," and "Hurry and hide under the trees." Shocked, we all rushed to take cover under a tree. At first we felt a bit anxious that we might not be able to take the ferry to Ie Island. Then we heard the sounds of bombs coming from the direction of Toguchi Harbor and we knew there was no choice but to give up going to Ie. We started the walk back on the road from which we came.

As we returned home, the air raid continued. When the aircraft came we would hide under trees and when the aircraft receded we would crawl out and started walking again. When I was a student I played volleyball and I was confident in my physical stamina. If it was just me, I knew I could run back home, but together with these two ladies, I was unable to hurry.

When we were very close to reaching home, another aircraft approached. We looked for somewhere to hide but we were in the middle of a rice field with no cover available. Then we ran back to a pine tree and hid underneath. After the aircraft passed we started walking along the river bank and the aircraft returned. On the river bank there were several mulberry trees but since they had lost their leaves they didn't provide much cover. Nonetheless I helped the two ladies hide under a mulberry tree and I clinged to the river bank and picked weeds to cover my face and body. I was desperate to remain unseen by the aircraft. But then the two ladies ran out from under the tree and came towards me crying, "It's so frightening!" I tried to hide them by frantically covering them with leaves. This scene of hiding from aircraft was repeated over and over and we finally got home at about five o'clock in the afternoon. We had been fleeing the air raid for the entire day.

Our neighborhood had suffered airstrikes and civil defense personnel were directing precautions against the attack. Our house was a mess and a dresser was left open. My mother was not there and it seemed she had left in a hurry. So I put a teacup in my bag went straight to the air raid shelter.

My mother had been so worried about me that she hadn't even eaten lunch. She was sitting at the entrance of the air raid shelter waiting for me

and immediately hugging me when I arrived. It was a long day of running.

The war begins

A while after the air raid, my father came back from Ie Island. For a time our day-to-day life was quiet and continued that way for a while so that we came to expect the war would not return to us.

However, one day the air raids started again.

(Note: On April 1, 1945, the U.S. military landed at the central west coast of the main island. On the 10th, the attack advanced to Nakijin Village.)

By then, it was too dangerous to stay in our home so we fled into the mountains to hide. The air raids grew increasingly fierce.

In the morning, bombardment from the warships start firing into the village with a loud, "Bang! Bang!" sound. By about three o'clock in the afternoon the shells continued up the mountain side with no break. Then suddenly is became quiet; almost as if there was no war. A lady came back from relieving herself and said to my mother, "The Japanese Army is here." Upon hearing this my mother felt we would be safe if the Japanese Army arrived. However, it was not Japanese soldiers, they were American soldiers.

After the bombardment stopped, the American military landed on the island. We were later told that since all the villagers had left, the Americans were able to move through the village with no difficulty.

The air raid shelter we made in the mountainside was different from the common shelter others made. My father had us add a side room with a vertical shaft. He also directed the arrangement of the interior of the shelter. We blocked off the entrance to the side room for added protection when hiding there. And, a tree was located at the entrance of the shelter to conceal the opening. In the shelter were my mother, my aunt, a few women, my cousins Shizuko and Akira, and seven more girls. Since Akira was four years old, I was always carrying him on my back. Shizuko was a

third grade student in elementary school. My father, very cautious against the enemy, usually guarded the entrance of the shelter out by the river bank.

Eventually the American soldiers discovered the entrance of our shelter. Three times they threw a hand grenade into the shelter. Then they burned dry tree branches in the entrance. Inside the shelter we all put our hands over our mouth so that we wouldn't inhale the smoke and we all kept quiet. Our eighty-year-old grandmother had been sleeping and not knowing what was going on, she woke up and started asking, "What's happening? What's happening?" Alarmed, there wasn't much we could do so we just covered her mouth with our hands.

My father was outside and saw the soldiers throw the hand grenades into the shelter. He thought everyone in the family must be dead and he was the only family member still alive. But, all of us in the shelter had hid in the side room and we escaped the direct impact from the blast. We stayed quiet inside the shelter and by evening we thought the U.S. soldiers must have left and we decided to go outside. I went outside first to see if it safe. After that, one by one, a crowd of people came out of the shelter. My father was overcome with joy as he watched us emerge and said in loud voice, "You all did so well!"

Refuge life in the mountains

My father was the head of the village district at the time. In preparation for emergencies, he placed the important village documents in a metal box hidden inside a stone wall. Even today, I clearly remember that after the war was over, everyone in the village was happy to see all the important documents were kept safe.

Our refugee life in the mountains continued. During the day we would hide in the mountains but when evening came there were no American military aircraft flying and we would descend the mountain and go back to the village to prepare food and wash. After finishing late at night, we would

go back up the mountain by early morning. Since I was in good physical shape I would go back and forth from the mountain to my house twice a day.

One day as we were headed back up the mountain, an American military aircraft flew by. If they saw us, we would be in danger of being fired upon by the aircraft's machine gun. I quickly hid under the nearest cycad tree. When I was holding the thorned trunk of the cycad tree, I was targeted and directly fired upon by the aircraft's machine gun. Bullets occasionally ripped through the leaves of the tree. When I heard an explosion on my right, I would run to the left; if I heard an explosion on the left, I would run to the right, thus circling around the cycad tree. My mother, crying, watched me targeted by the bombs from further up the mountain. My father stared unblinking from higher up. While I was running back and forth, not knowing what to do, the aircraft eventually flew off. Seeing me emerge from under the cycad tree, my relieved father exclaimed, "Tsuru is okay!" I acted calm and carried a basket slowly down the mountain while maintaining my composure. This was my most terrifying war experience.

The battle was over not long after that. American soldiers announced in broken Japanese on a megaphone, "The war is over. Everything is okay now. Please go home." At first we didn't believe this and thought we would be killed if we went outside so we didn't return home. We girls were told that if you were caught by American soldiers, you would be assaulted. My father made a hiding place in a patch of tall ferns just big enough for one person and I hid there alone.

Once, a U.S. soldier came back to the mountain. I hid in some ferns and watched as he approached my father. My father was sure if he was apprehended he would be killed. As the soldier approached, he took a Japanese flag from his pocket and laid it on the ground. Then my father stomped on the flag and the U.S. soldier laughed and patted him on the shoulder. My father sincerely regretted this disrespect to Japan even long after the war. Occasionally he would mention this incident and my mother would try to cheer him up by saying, "If you hadn't stepped on the flag,

you would probably not be alive today." In the evening after this incident, the soldiers left the area and we decided we would come down from the mountain and return home the next day.

Hiding day after day from the American soldiers

After we came back from the mountain I didn't want to be seen by American soldiers so I stayed hidden by myself in the loft of a shed that was separated from the main house. I ate in the loft, and only came down at night. Urged by others who thought I must be lonely staying so isolated, after about a month I moved from the shed into the attic of the main house.

At that time several people who had evacuated from their homes were living together with us in our house. There wasn't any work or much to do so we spent our days talking about our experiences on the mountainside and chatting. My father felt pity for me living alone in the attic and poked holes in the door of the cabinet below the family alter to make a small room for me where I could stay and interact with others. I spent three months living that way. My friends heard that I was still in hiding and came to see me saying, "It's alright; you can come out now." Finally, I came out from hiding.

Still though, when we went outside we were careful not to be noticed as young women. We used soot from the bottom of a pan and oil to make a dark cream and we disguised ourselves by dirtying our faces. One day as I was helping my mother wash potatoes, two U.S. soldiers approached. It was the first time I had seen an American soldier up close. I pretended I didn't noticed them and turned away, tossing potatoes into a basket. As the soldiers approached and saw my blackened face, they both laughed loudly. Then they poured the water into the washbowl and gestured for me to wash my face. I gave in to their request and quickly washed my face. After seeing me wash my face they smiled and left. I had been so frightened every day but now I thought to myself that among the Americans there

were good people like those two soldiers. From that time on I was able to go about my day without hiding.

I have not wanted to talk about the frightened things that happened during the war and never mentioned it to kids. Actually, I wish I could erase all my memories of the war. At first I was hesitant to talk about the war but then I thought if I didn't, I would come to regret it, and so I decided to tell my story.

Unless you personally experience it, you probably cannot understand the true agony of war. However, when you think about the war, please think of me. Please think about the story that I shared today. I am now 94 years old. Though many years and months have passed, even today I can never forgot what happened during the war when I was 19 years old.

After the Interview Mizuki Yonaha

Upon hearing Ms. Tsuru's war experience, one part of the story that most impressed upon my heart was when the American soldiers threw hand grenades into the air shelter. The shelter was created by her father and rather than just a straight tunnel leading to the room, he designed a winding entrance inside the shelter. When the grenade was throw into the shelter, Ms. Tsuru had to cover her mouth with her hands while hiding beyond the winding tunnel. Just thinking about it makes me scared and those who lived through it like Ms. Tsuru must have been more scared.

I have heard many other war experiences but I think Ms. Tsuru is such an amazing person having been so young while leading others to safety in the midst of war. In order to survive she overcame her own mental and physical challenges and pulled others through to escape. She was truly brave and I don't think I would be able to do the same.

I was so impressed by the leadership and brave action Ms. Tsuru displayed to protect others under the harsh conditions of war. I think a person with true leadership skills is able to understand the diverse viewpoints of others

and work together as a team.

War is cruel. I think to myself that we must never repeat war. Since I have not directly experienced war I may not be able to grasp the true meaning nor the horror or pain. Still, I can tell the next generation what I have learned listening to these war experiences. This is what I can do for the future.

Never forgetting Ms. Tsuru's valuable, personal war experience, I want to think about how to pass her story on to many other people. Also I want to compare Ms. Tsuru's story with my grandmother's story about evacuation during the war.

I feel it is important to value my grandmother's experiences during the war and her expectations for the future of the world. I want to personally contribute to the cause of peace and take action for a better future. My individual actions may be a small cause, but continuous progress is important.

In Closing

The Soka Gakkai Okinawa Youth Division has been engaged in a peace movement for some time now. One of our goals has been to instill the next generation with a "peace movement for the future." One campaign to bring this about was to have Okinawa Future Division members interview survivors of the Battle of Okinawa and hear their experiences firsthand. This project comes to fruition in the form of this book.

In 2016, a book of interviews by the Youth Division titled *Thinking Peace for the Future, True Stories from 14 Survivors* was published. For this new book, the focus was on junior and senior high school students who will be responsible for a new era in Okinawa. Seventy-five years have passed since the war, and as the time draws near when there will be none left to share their war experiences, the members of this group of junior and senior high school students will pass on these experiences of the Battle of Okinawa. It was most significant that they were able to meet with and hear directly from these survivors. Through this book, we hope that the young people who carry the future of Okinawa will be able to feel the "kukuru (heart) of Okinawa" as they strive for peace. Our great hope is this feeling will be passed on to future generations.

In 2018, the Okinawa Youth Division held the "World Youth Peace Culture Festival" at the Okinawa Convention Center where 15,000 people, mostly young people, gathered for the event. There are many traditional Okinawan phrases passed down from our ancestors which symbolize the spirit of Okinawa. Examples include "Life is a treasure," "Care for others," "Once we have met, we are brothers and sisters" and "Help one another." At the festival, the deep spiritual meaning of these words was employed by the youth of Okinawa to bring people together where they pledged to join hands with one another, transcending all differences with a "union of the heart," connecting their hearts and minds.

The Future Division members who became the center of this campaign to conduct interviews of the survivors of the Battle of Okinawa participated in that Peace Cultural Festival. Additionally, in order further spread the story of

the Battle of Okinawa to future generations we are producing a pictorial story exhibition based on these testimonies of the war in Okinawa.

We should not let the "memory of war" fade away, but instead we must try to keep the "spirit of peace" in Okinawa alive into the future. We are at a crossroads of whether or not we can achieve this. Now is the time to convey the importance of peace to the younger generation, and we, the Youth Division, are determined to continue this movement to develop together.

SGI President Ikeda visited Okinawa for the first time 60 years ago in July 1960. He visited the site of the war in the south. Seeing the scars of the war, he said, "Okinawa, which has suffered the most, has the right to be the happiest and most peaceful place." It was with this in mind that he began writing his novel, *The Human Revolution*, in Okinawa.

The theme of *The Human Revolution* is: "A great human revolution in just a single individual will help achieve a change in the destiny of a nation." This is a philosophy that can achieve our goal of building peace, "and further, will enable a change in the destiny of all humankind." We, the young people who have received the baton of President Ikeda's "Pledge of No War," will carry out sincere dialogue and take concrete actions in our own regions. Our first step toward world peace is to encourage successors who will be the main actors in peacebuilding. We will continue to spread the struggle for peace throughout Japan and the world.

Finally, we would like to express our sincere thanks to Daisanbunmei-sha for their efforts in publishing this book, to all those who have shared their experiences in the war with the Okinawa Future Division, the Okinawa Youth Peace Committee, and the Women's Peace Culture Conference for their support.

June 2020

Tsunehito Maejima
Soka Gakkai Okinawa Youth Division Leader